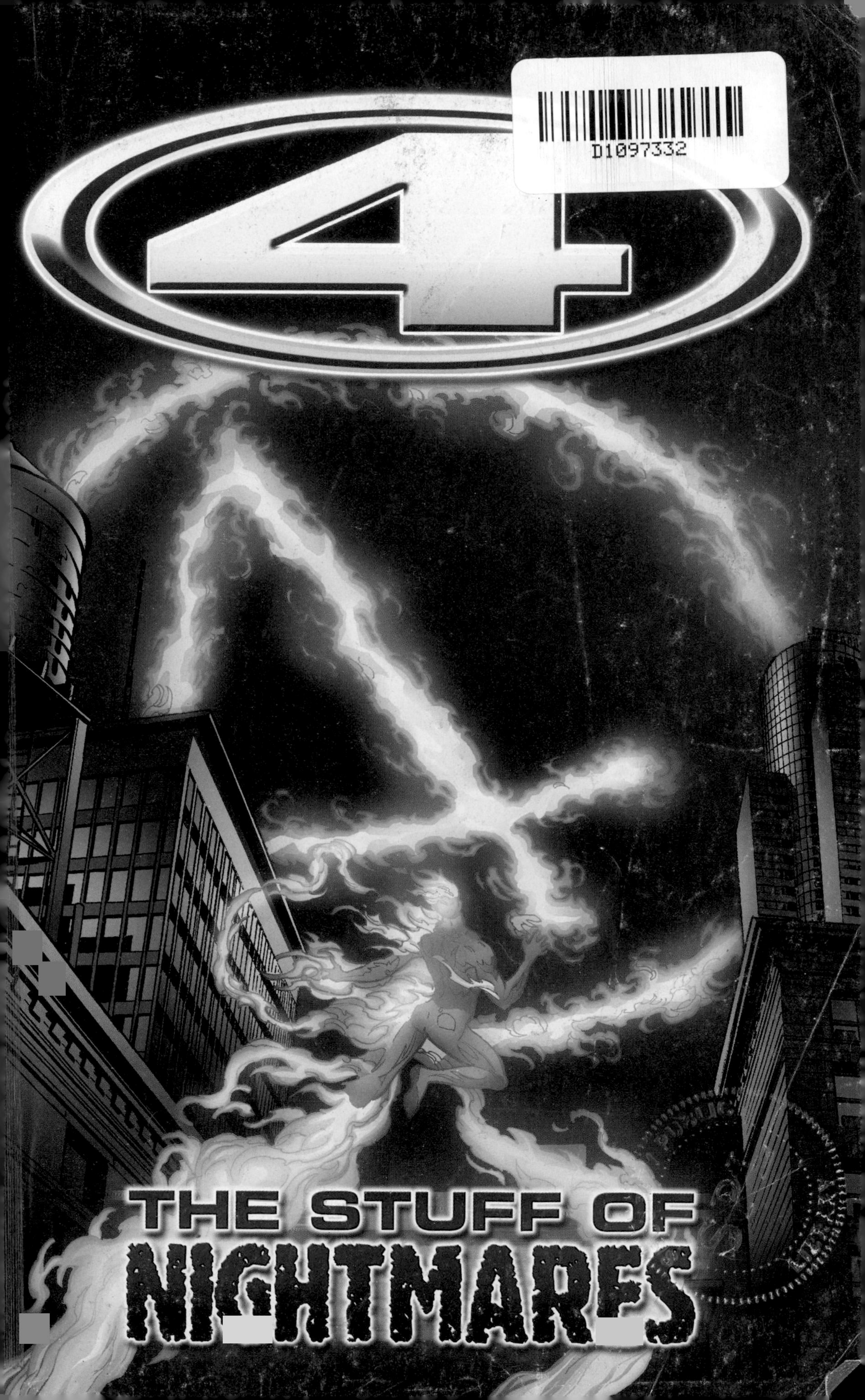
4
THE STUFF OF
NIGHTMARES

4

THE STUFF OF NIGHTMARES

Writer:
Roberto Aguirre-Sacasa

Penciler:
Jim Muniz
with Staz Johnson (ISSUE #11)

Inkers:
Scott Hanna
(Issue #10: Breakdowns by Jim Muniz & Finishes by Scott Hanna)

Colorists:
Brian Reber
with Morry Hollowell (Issue #8) & Sotocolor's J. Brown (Issue #9)

Letterers:
**Virtual Calligraphy's Randy Gentile,
Cory Petit & Dave Sharpe**

Cover Artist:
Steve McNiven

Editor:
Warren Simons

Executive Editor:
Axel Alonso

Collections Editor:
Jeff Youngquist

Assistant Editor:
Jennifer Grünwald

Book Designer:
Patrick McGrath

Creative Director:
Tom Marvelli

Editor in Chief:
Joe Quesada

Publisher:
Dan Buckley

Appearing in Issue #10, the character COUNT GORE DE VOL is owned by Dick Dyszel
www.countgore.com

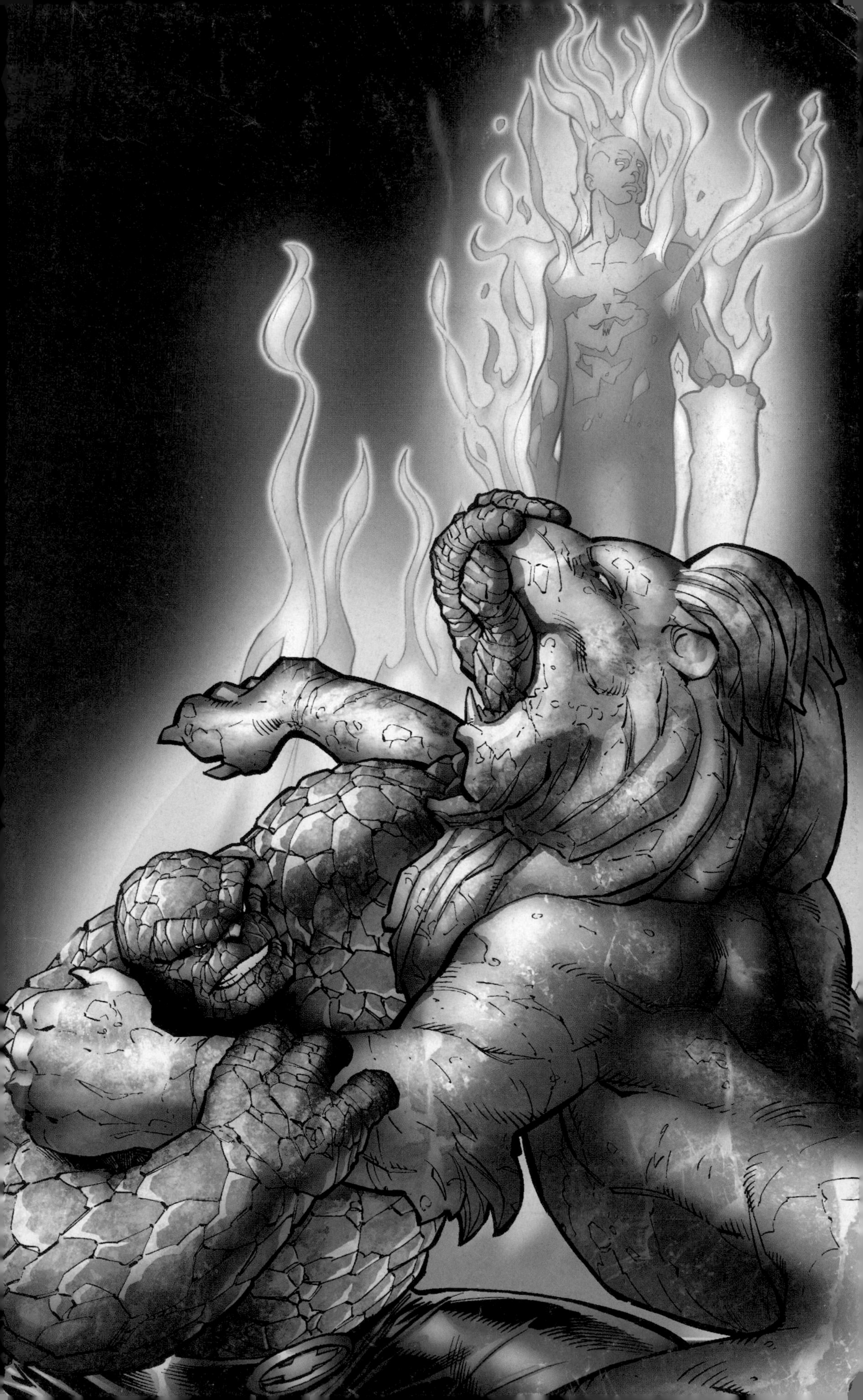

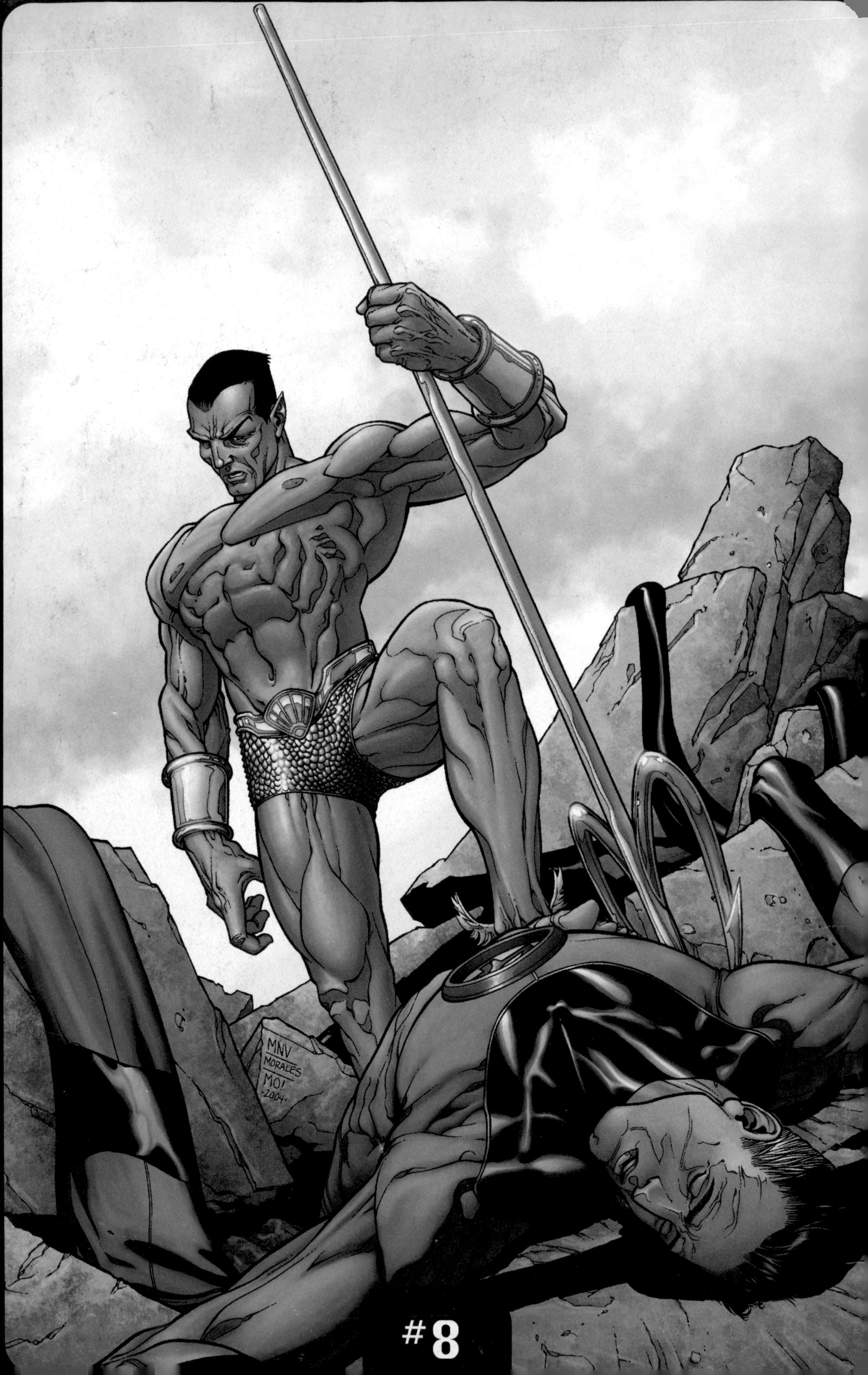
MNV
MORALES
MO!
2004

#8

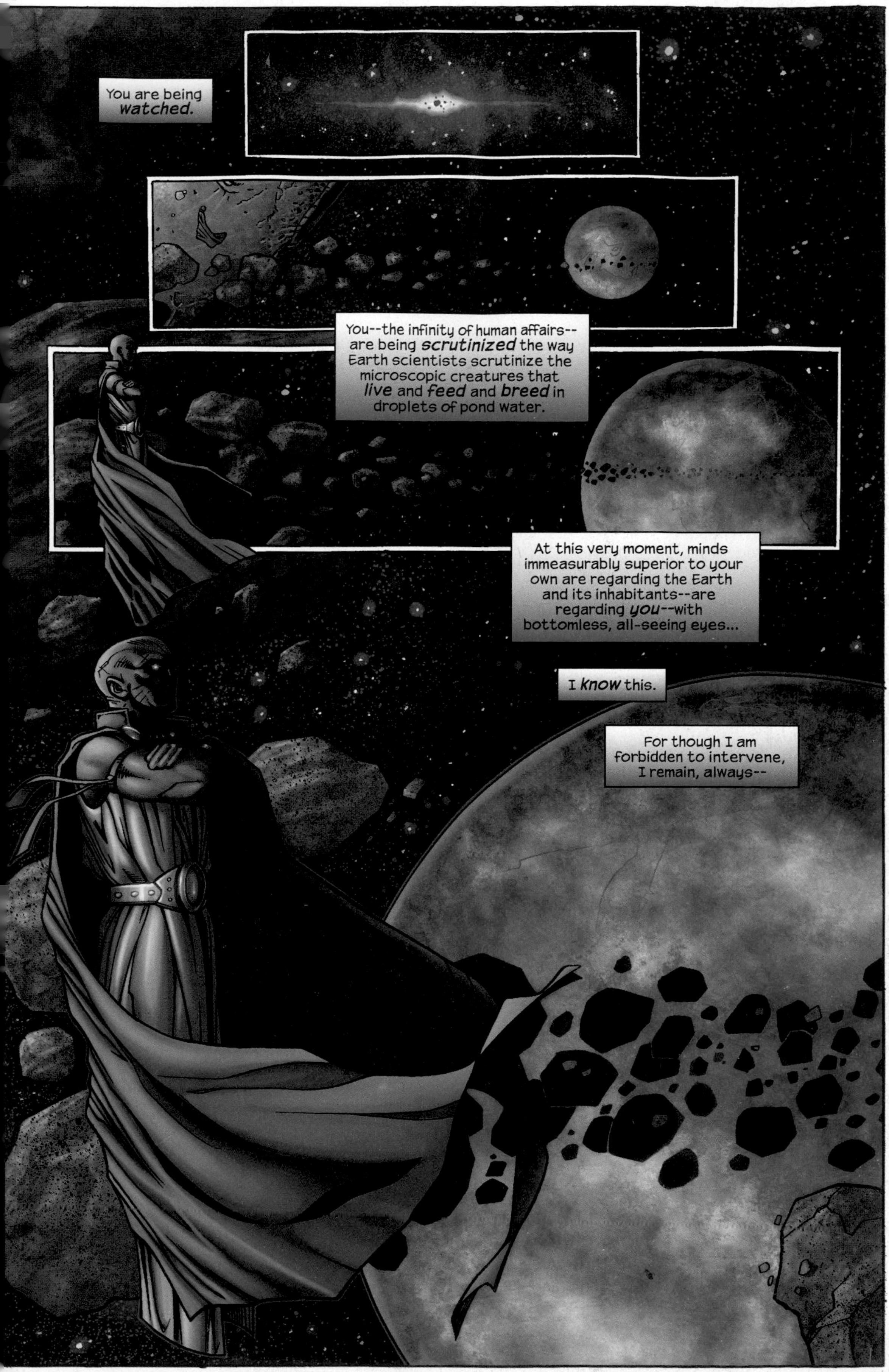
You are being watched.
You--the infinity of human affairs--are being scrutinized the way Earth scientists scrutinize the microscopic creatures that live and feed and breed in droplets of pond water.
At this very moment, minds immeasurably superior to your own are regarding the Earth and its inhabitants--are regarding you--with bottomless, all-seeing eyes...
I know this.
For though I am forbidden to intervene, I remain, always--

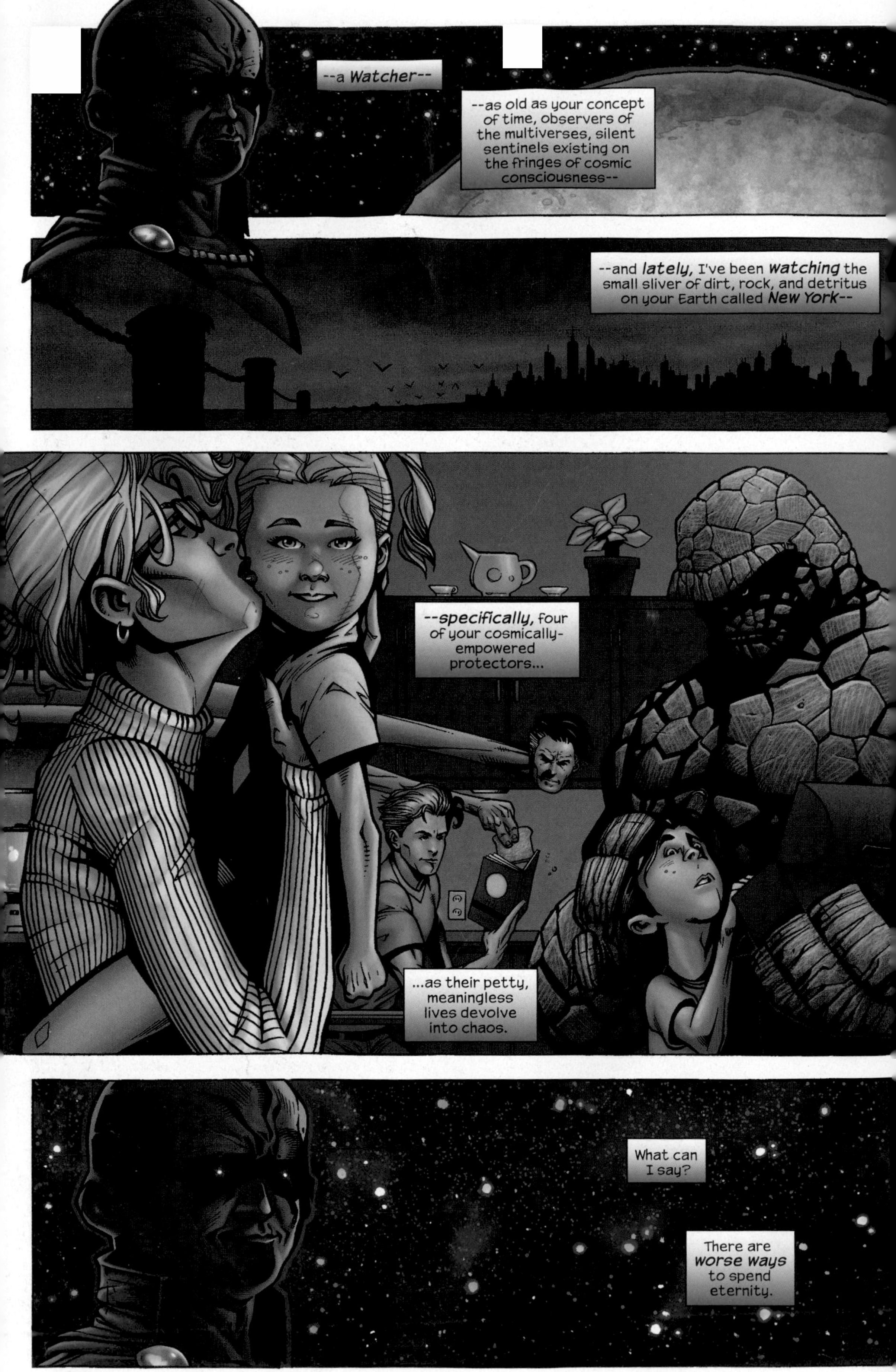
--a Watcher--
--as old as your concept of time, observers of the multiverses, silent sentinels existing on the fringes of cosmic consciousness--
--and lately, I've been watching the small sliver of dirt, rock, and detritus on your Earth called New York--
--specifically, four of your cosmically-empowered protectors...
...as their petty, meaningless lives devolve into chaos.
What can I say?
There are worse ways to spend eternity.

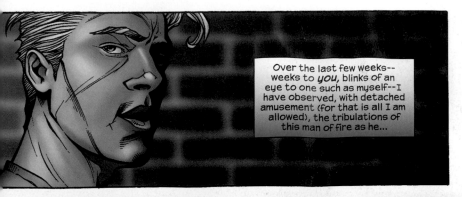

Over the last few weeks-- weeks to *you,* blinks of an eye to one such as myself--I have observed, with detached amusement (for that is all I am allowed), the tribulations of this man of fire as he...

...well, *see* for yourself.

¿Whew?

Finally.

Man, if I have to *mop* one more floor...

Oh--uh-- hey, guys, what's up? How was...

...lunch?

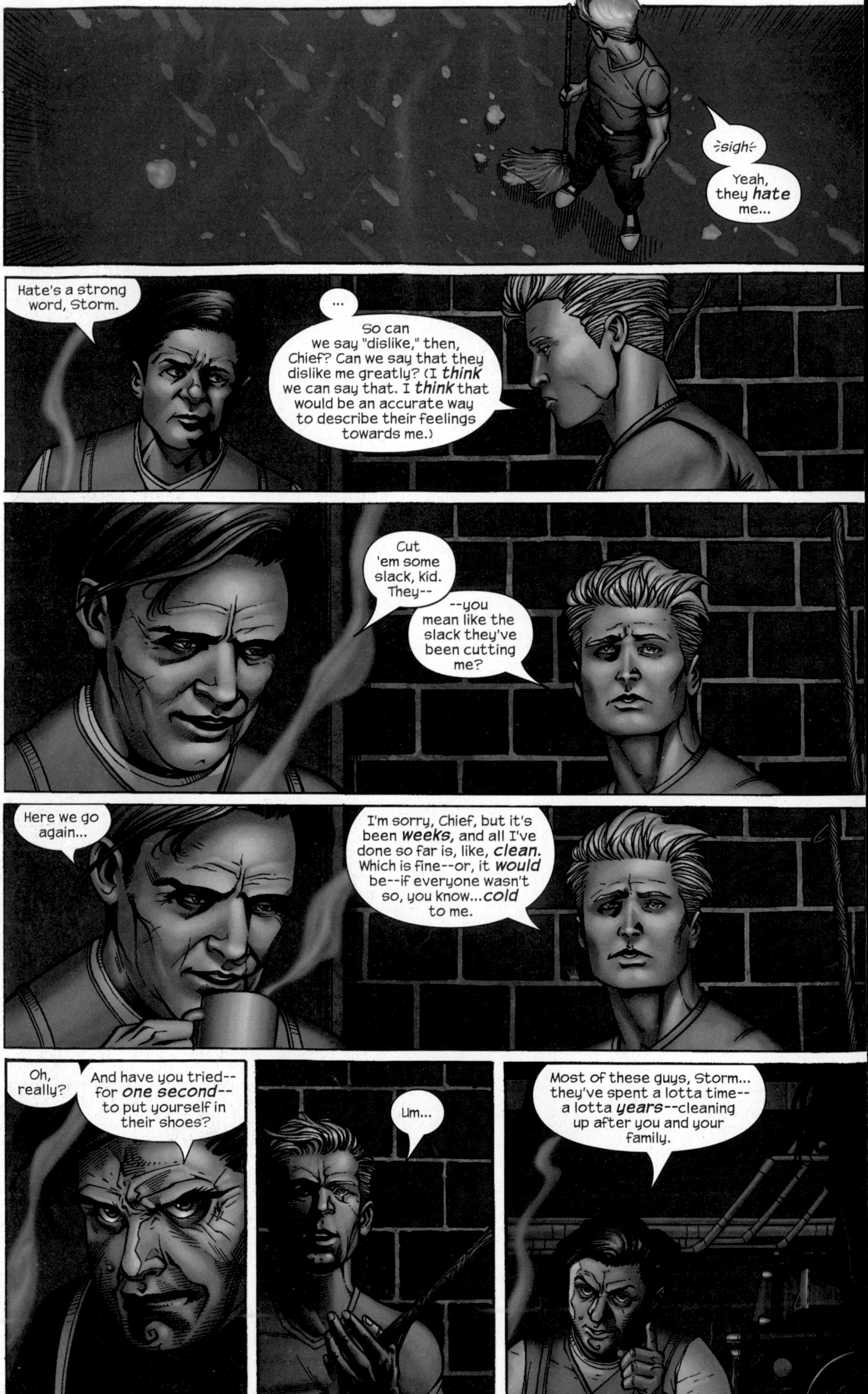

-sigh-
Yeah, they hate me...
Hate's a strong word, Storm.
...
So can we say "dislike," then, Chief? Can we say that they dislike me greatly? (I think we can say that. I think that would be an accurate way to describe their feelings towards me.)
Cut 'em some slack, kid. They--
--you mean like the slack they've been cutting me?
Here we go again...
I'm sorry, Chief, but it's been weeks, and all I've done so far is, like, clean. Which is fine--or, it would be--if everyone wasn't so, you know...cold to me.
Oh, really?
And have you tried--for one second--to put yourself in their shoes?
Um...
Most of these guys, Storm... they've spent a lotta time--a lotta years--cleaning up after you and your family.

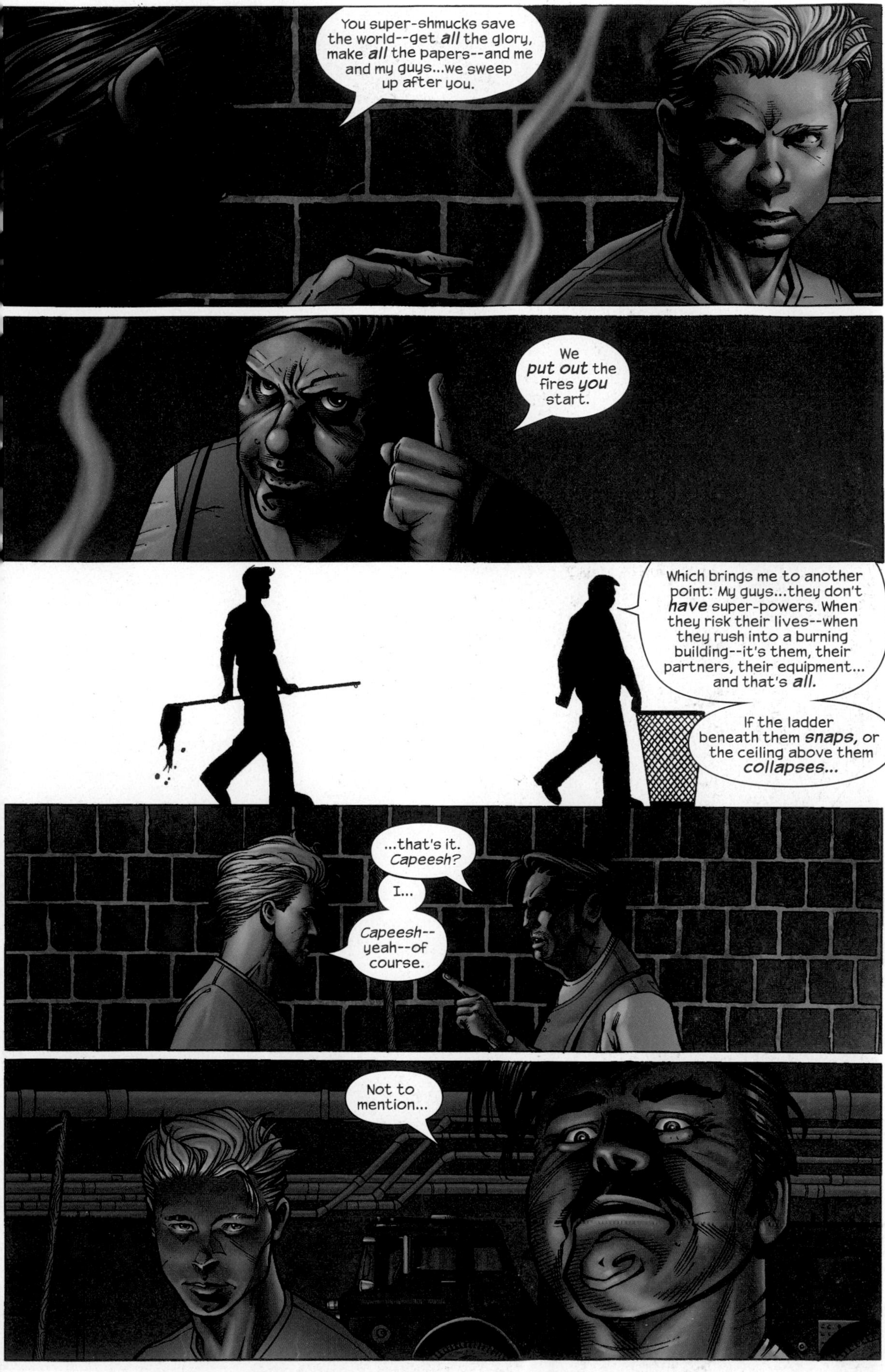
You super-shmucks save the world--get all the glory, make all the papers--and me and my guys...we sweep up after you.
We put out the fires you start.
Which brings me to another point: My guys...they don't have super-powers. When they risk their lives--when they rush into a burning building--it's them, their partners, their equipment... and that's all.
If the ladder beneath them snaps, or the ceiling above them collapses...
...that's it. Capeesh?
I...
Capeesh--yeah--of course.
Not to mention...

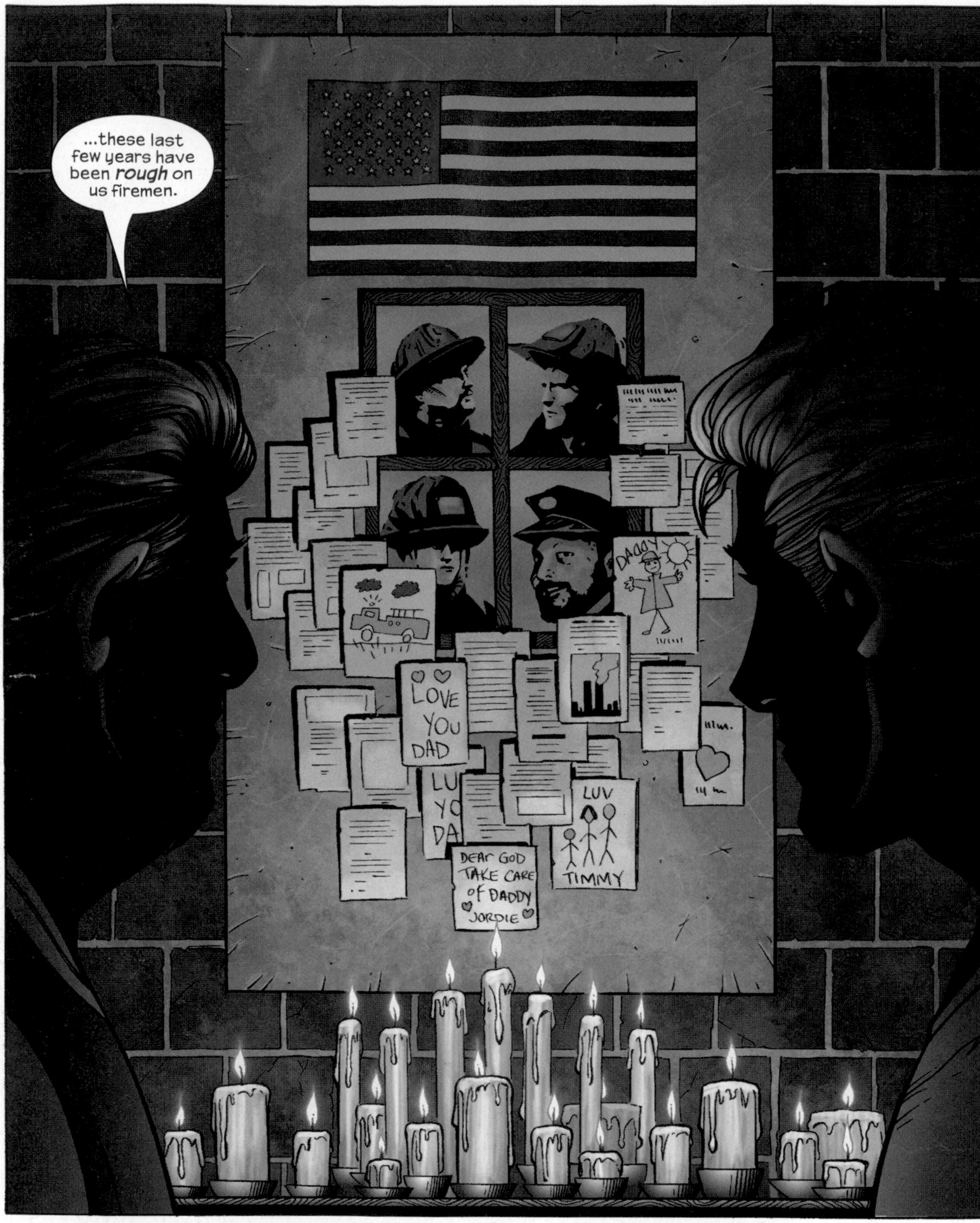
...these last few years have been *rough* on us firemen.
LOVE YOU DAD
LUV YO DA
DEAR GOD TAKE CARE OF DADDY JORDIE
LUV TIMMY
DADDY

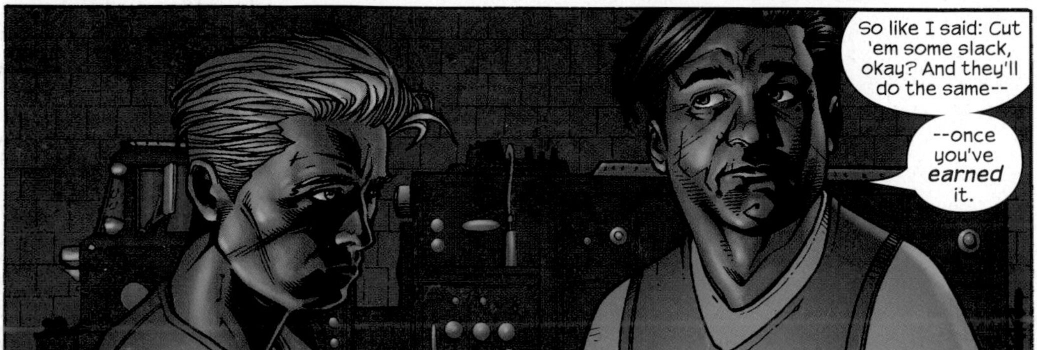
So like I said: Cut 'em some slack, okay? And they'll do the same--
--once you've *earned* it.

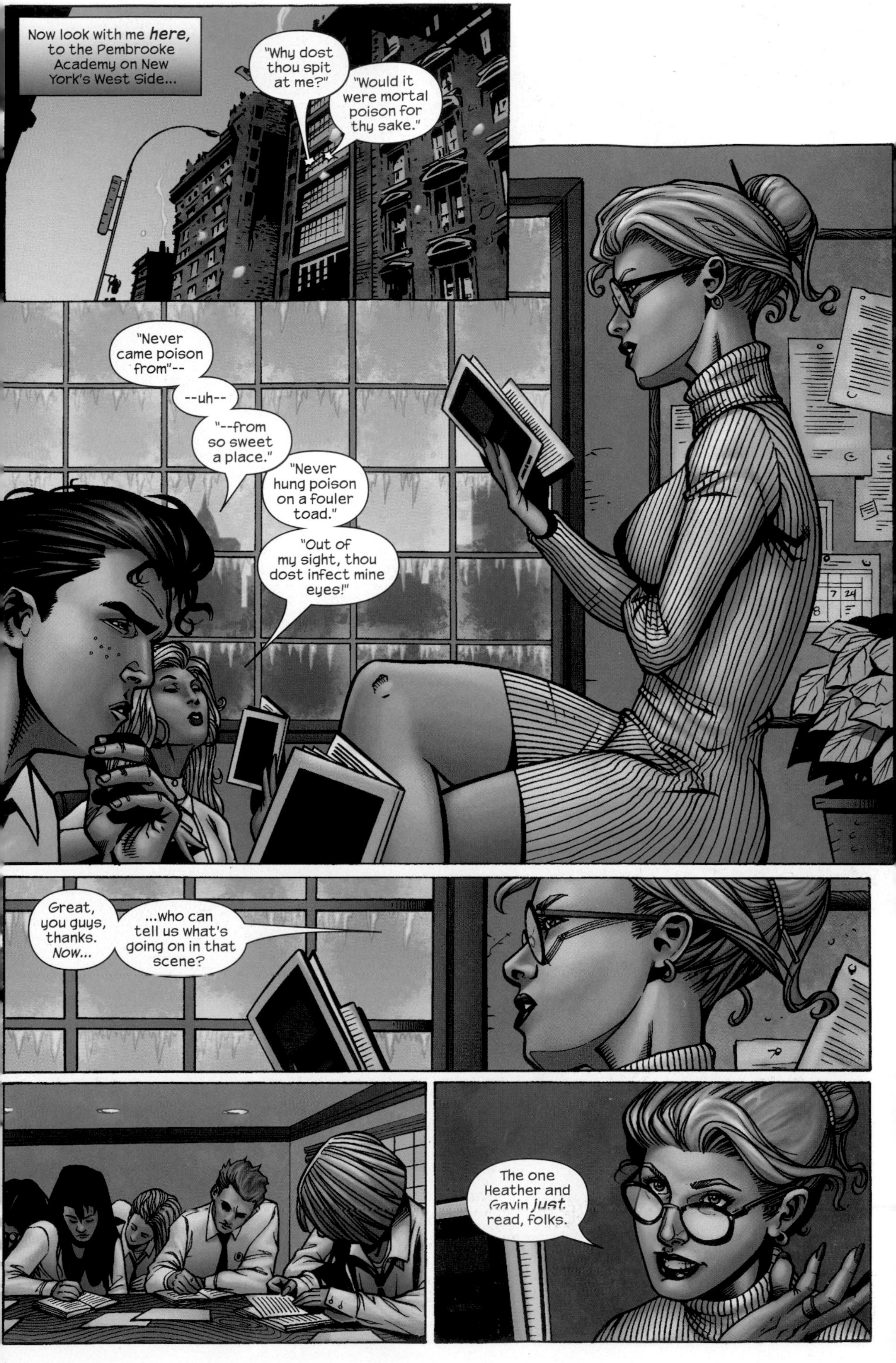

Now look with me here, to the Pembrooke Academy on New York's West Side...
"Why dost thou spit at me?"
"Would it were mortal poison for thy sake."
"Never came poison from"--
--uh--
"--from so sweet a place."
"Never hung poison on a fouler toad."
"Out of my sight, thou dost infect mine eyes!"
Great, you guys, thanks. Now...
...who can tell us what's going on in that scene?
The one Heather and Gavin just read, folks.

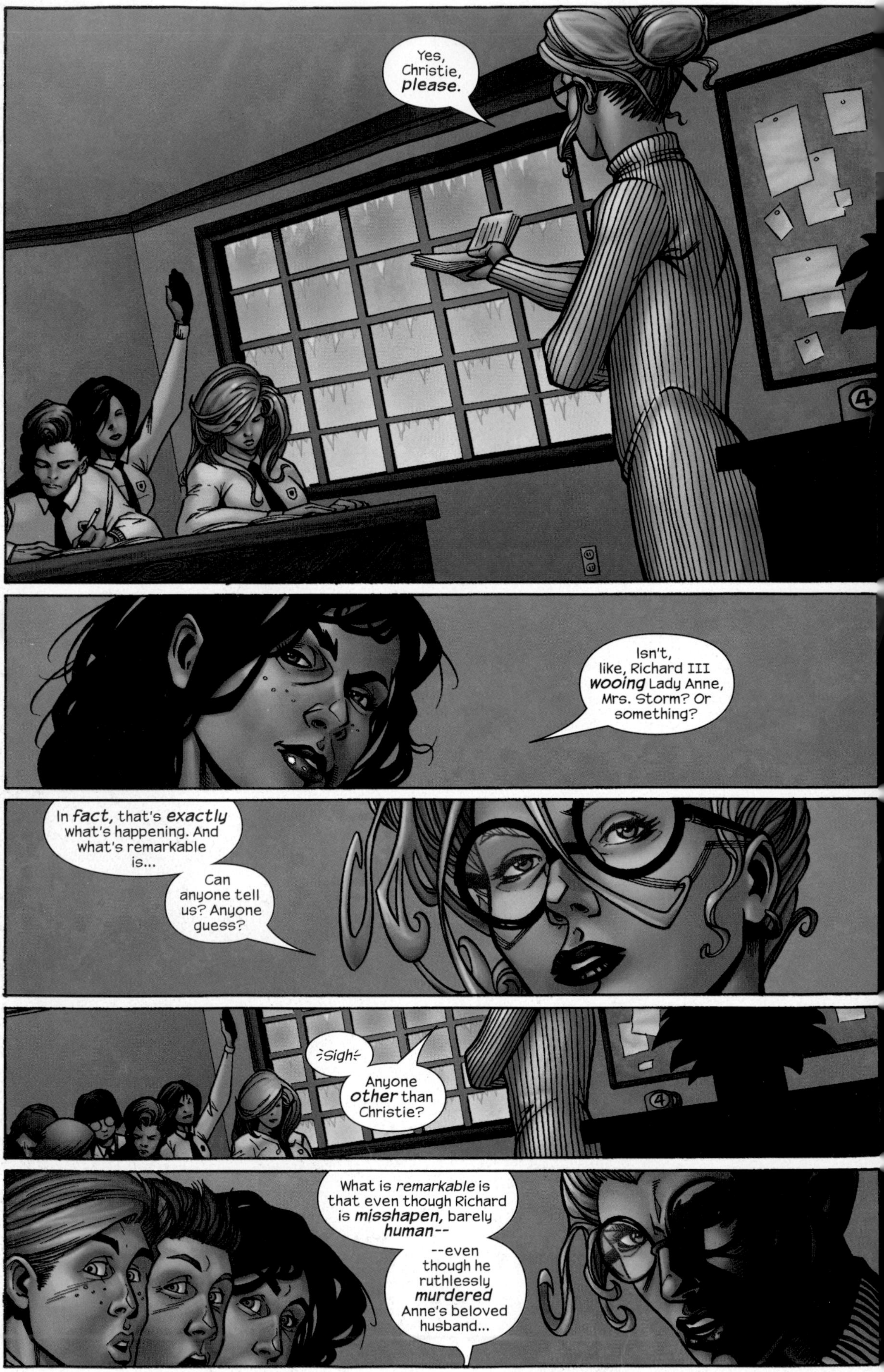
Yes, Christie, *please.*
Isn't, like, Richard III *wooing* Lady Anne, Mrs. Storm? Or something?
In *fact,* that's *exactly* what's happening. And what's remarkable is...
Can anyone tell us? Anyone guess?
Sigh
Anyone *other* than Christie?
What is *remarkable* is that even though Richard is *misshapen,* barely *human*--
--even though he ruthlessly *murdered* Anne's beloved husband...

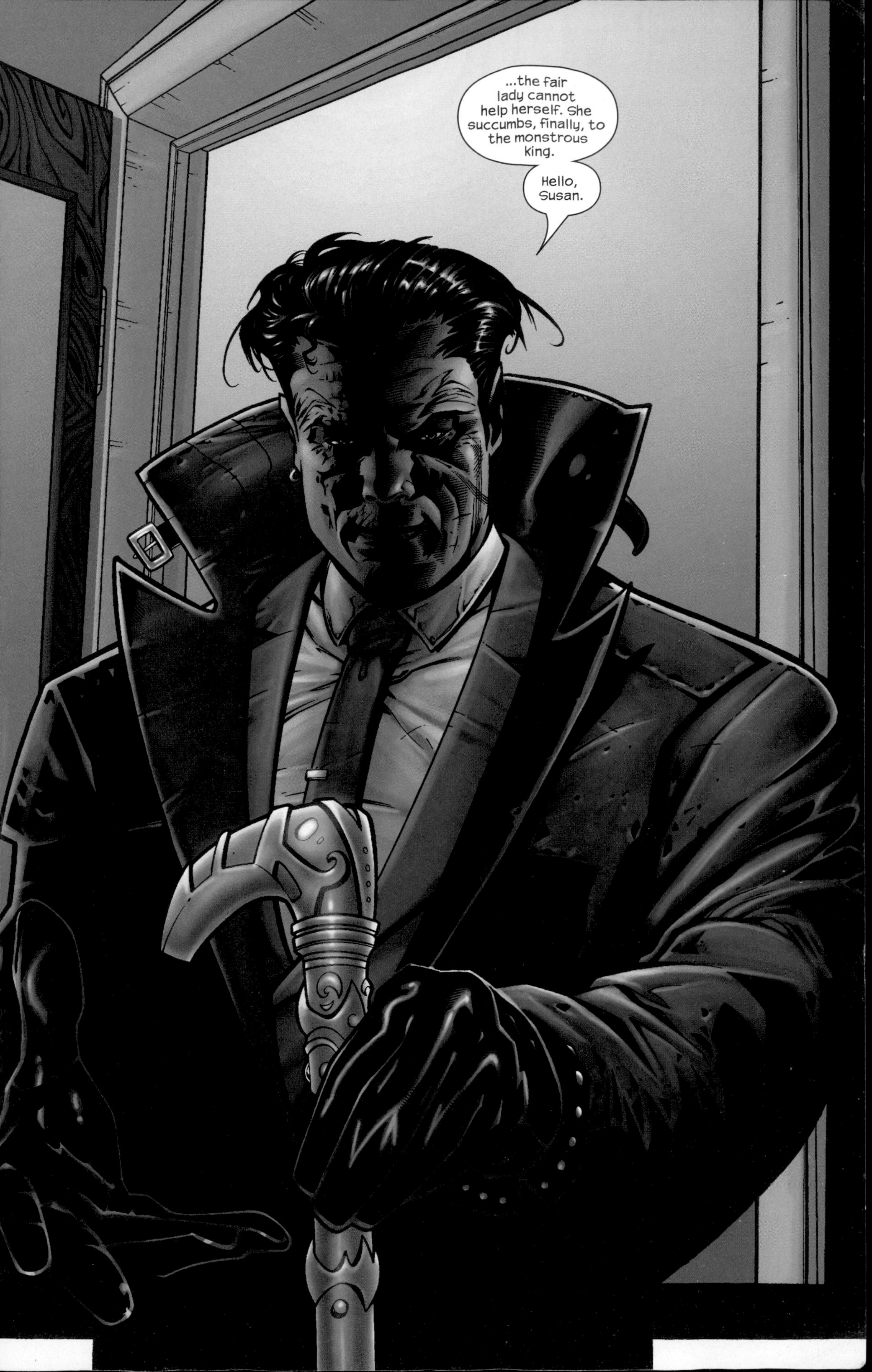
...the fair lady cannot help herself. She succumbs, finally, to the monstrous king.
Hello, Susan.

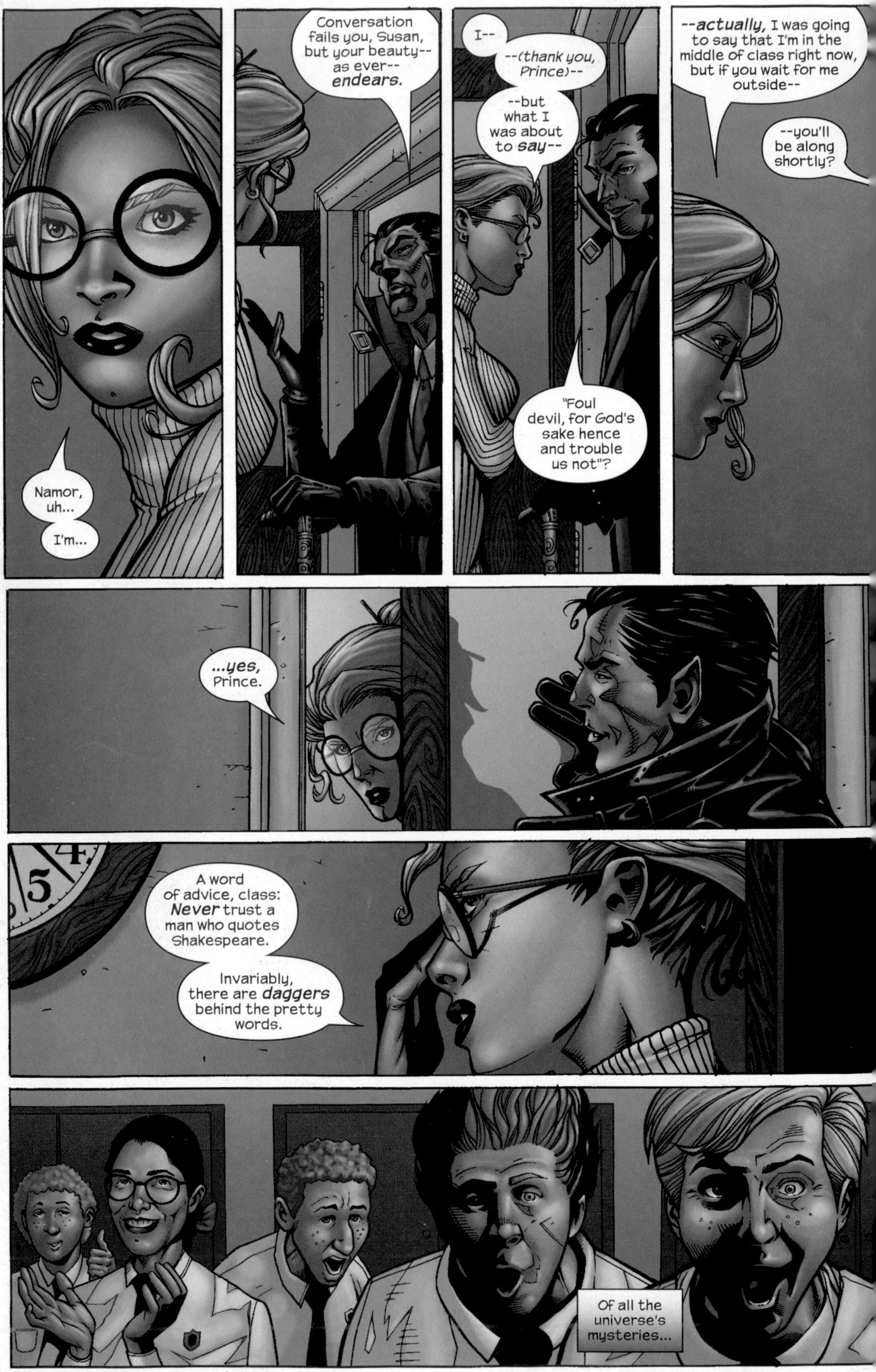
Namor, uh...
I'm...
Conversation fails you, Susan, but your beauty-- as ever-- endears.
I--
--(thank you, Prince)--
--but what I was about to say--
"Foul devil, for God's sake hence and trouble us not"?
--actually, I was going to say that I'm in the middle of class right now, but if you wait for me outside--
--you'll be along shortly?
...yes, Prince.
A word of advice, class: Never trust a man who quotes Shakespeare.
Invariably, there are daggers behind the pretty words.
Of all the universe's mysteries...

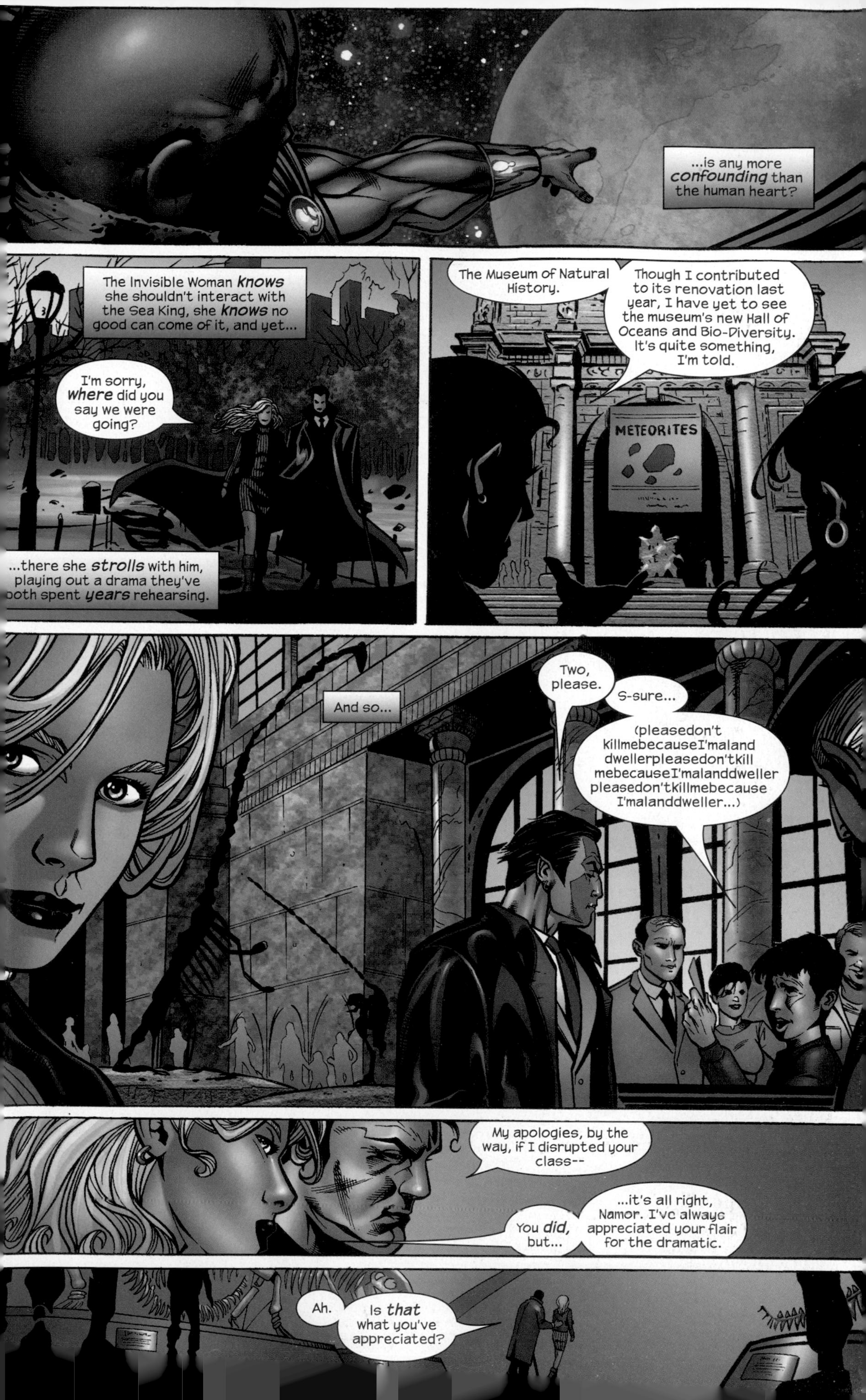
...is any more confounding than the human heart?
The Invisible Woman knows she shouldn't interact with the Sea King, she knows no good can come of it, and yet...
I'm sorry, where did you say we were going?
...there she strolls with him, playing out a drama they've both spent years rehearsing.
The Museum of Natural History.
Though I contributed to its renovation last year, I have yet to see the museum's new Hall of Oceans and Bio-Diversity. It's quite something, I'm told.
METEORITES
And so...
Two, please.
S-sure...
(pleasedon't killmebecauseI'maland dwellerpleasedon'tkill mebecauseI'malanddweller pleasedon'tkillmebecause I'malanddweller...)
My apologies, by the way, if I disrupted your class--
You did, but...
...it's all right, Namor. I've always appreciated your flair for the dramatic.
Ah.
Is that what you've appreciated?

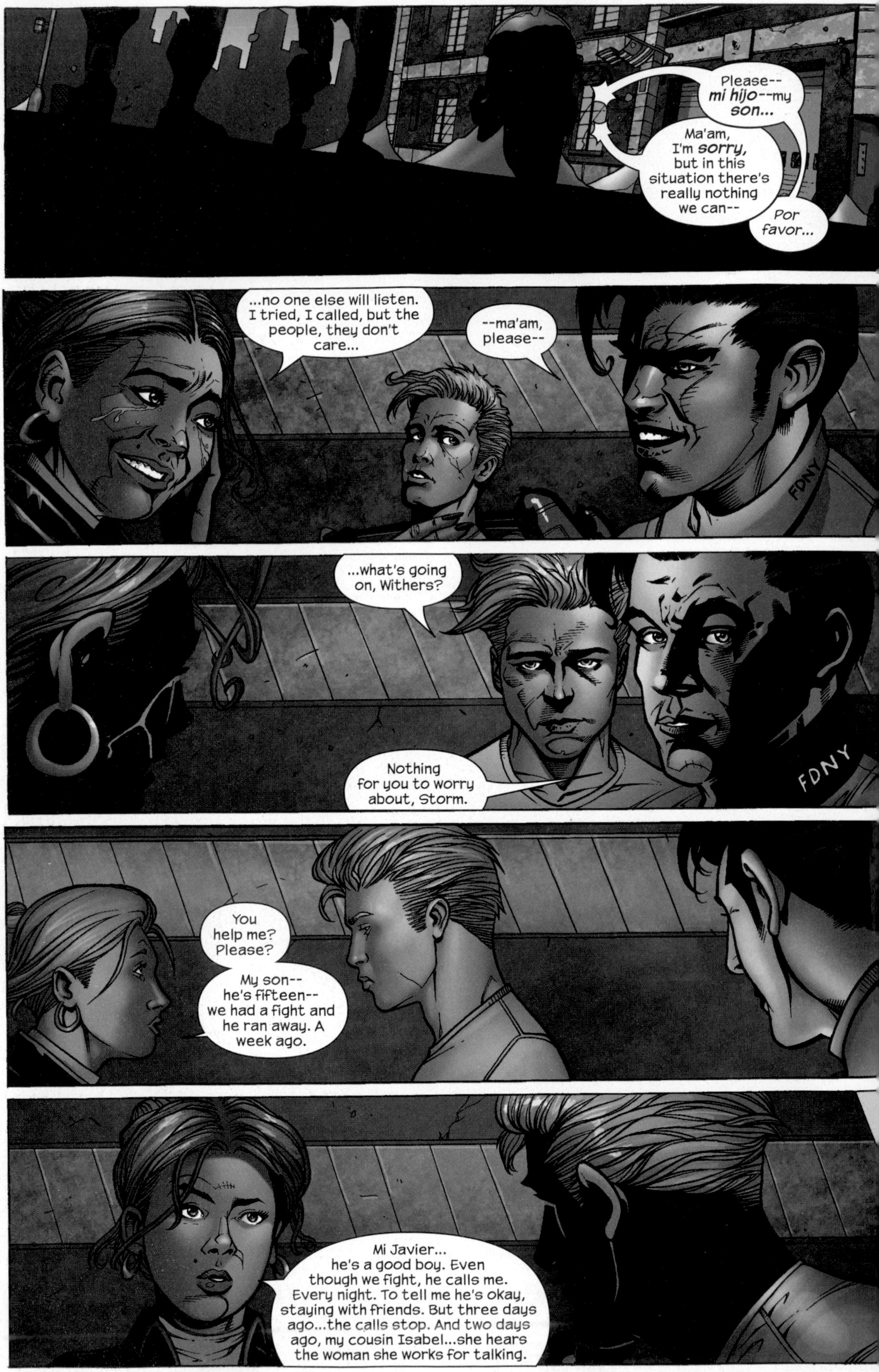
Please-- mi hijo--my son...
Ma'am, I'm sorry, but in this situation there's really nothing we can--
Por favor...
...no one else will listen. I tried, I called, but the people, they don't care...
--ma'am, please--
FDNY
...what's going on, Withers?
Nothing for you to worry about, Storm.
FDNY
You help me? Please?
My son-- he's fifteen-- we had a fight and he ran away. A week ago.
Mi Javier... he's a good boy. Even though we fight, he calls me. Every night. To tell me he's okay, staying with friends. But three days ago...the calls stop. And two days ago, my cousin Isabel...she hears the woman she works for talking.

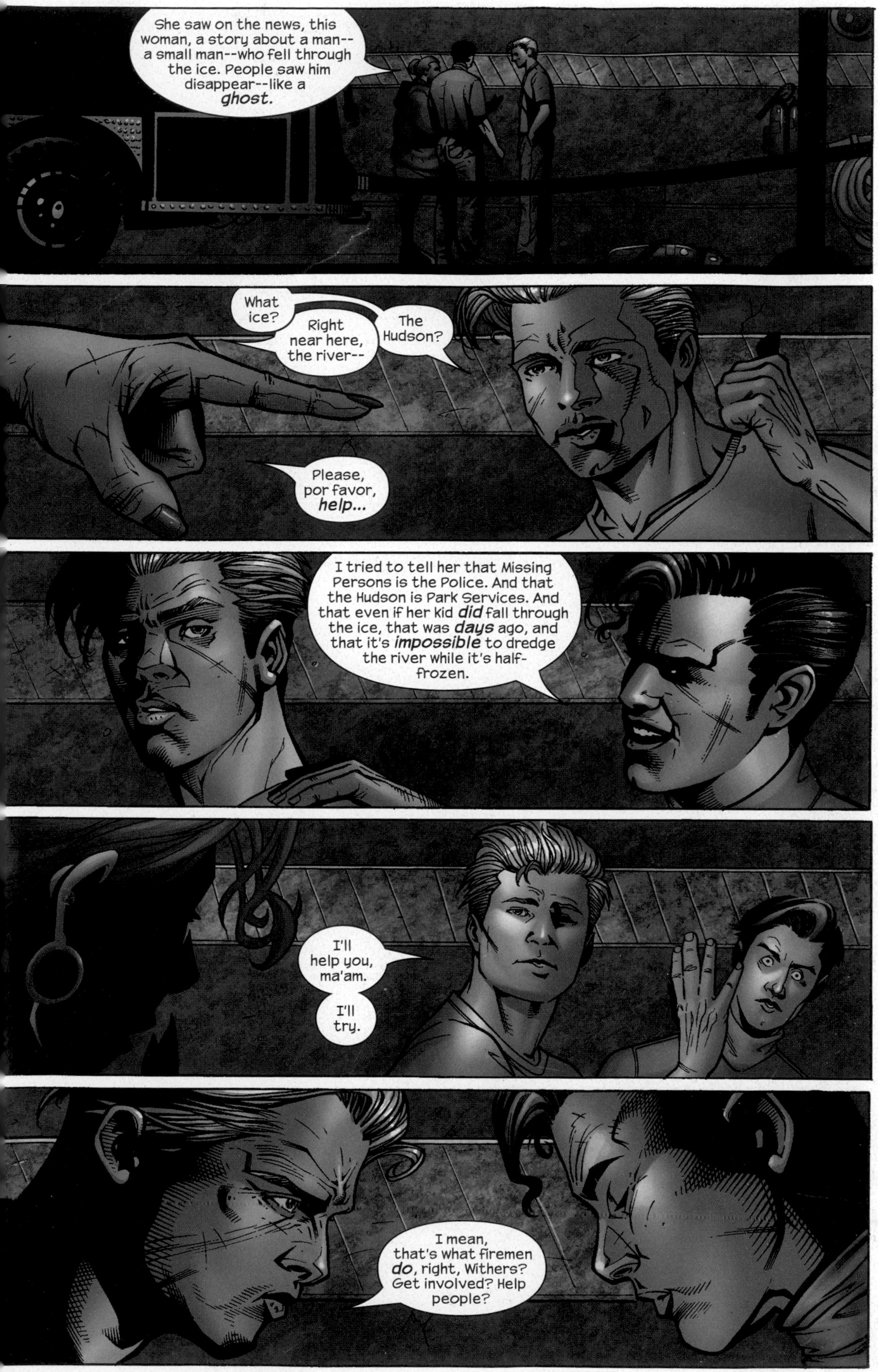
She saw on the news, this woman, a story about a man-- a small man--who fell through the ice. People saw him disappear--like a *ghost.*
What ice?
Right near here, the river--
The Hudson?
Please, por favor, *help...*
I tried to tell her that Missing Persons is the Police. And that the Hudson is Park Services. And that even if her kid *did* fall through the ice, that was *days* ago, and that it's *impossible* to dredge the river while it's half-frozen.
I'll help you, ma'am.
I'll try.
I mean, that's what firemen *do*, right, Withers? Get involved? Help people?

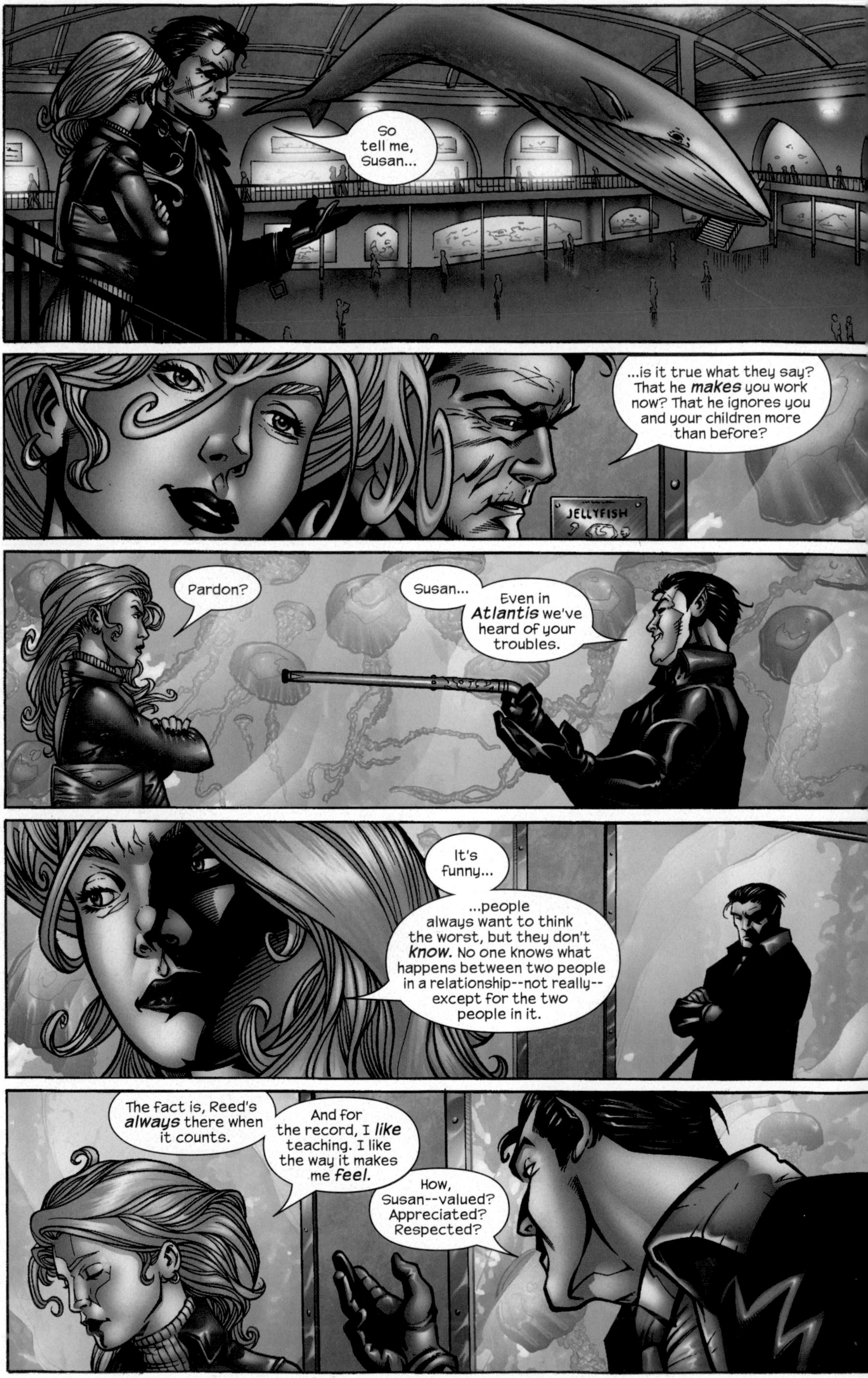

So tell me, Susan...
...is it true what they say? That he *makes* you work now? That he ignores you and your children more than before?
JELLYFISH
Pardon?
Susan...
Even in *Atlantis* we've heard of your troubles.
It's funny...
...people always want to think the worst, but they don't *know.* No one knows what happens between two people in a relationship--not really--except for the two people in it.
The fact is, Reed's *always* there when it counts.
And for the record, I *like* teaching. I like the way it makes me *feel.*
How, Susan--valued? Appreciated? Respected?

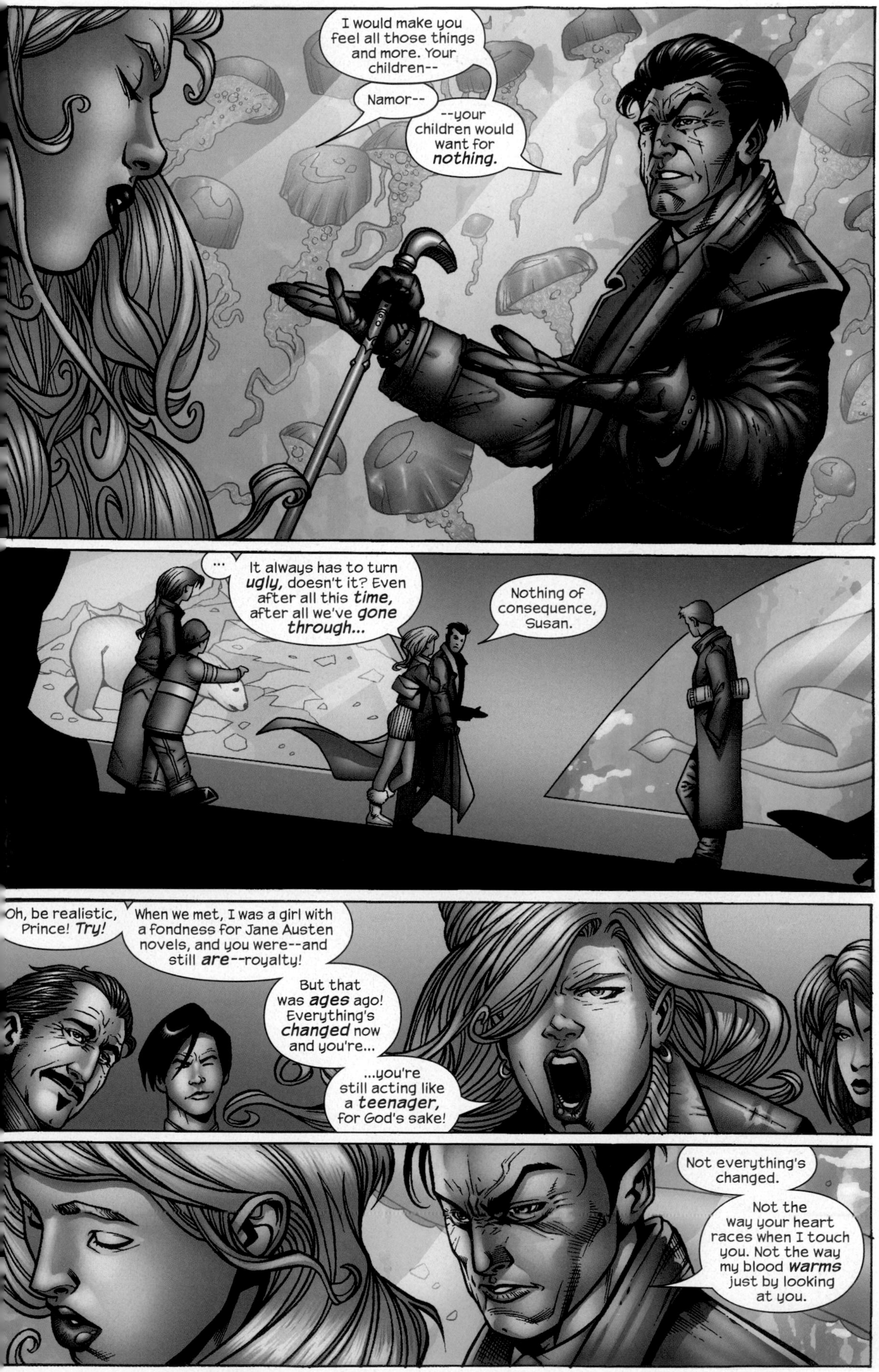

I would make you feel all those things and more. Your children--
Namor--
--your children would want for *nothing.*
...
It always has to turn *ugly,* doesn't it? Even after all this *time,* after all we've *gone through...*
Nothing of consequence, Susan.
Oh, be realistic, Prince! *Try!*
When we met, I was a girl with a fondness for Jane Austen novels, and you were--and still *are*--royalty!
But that was *ages* ago! Everything's *changed* now and you're...
...you're still acting like a *teenager,* for God's sake!
Not everything's changed.
Not the way your heart races when I touch you. Not the way my blood *warms* just by looking at you.

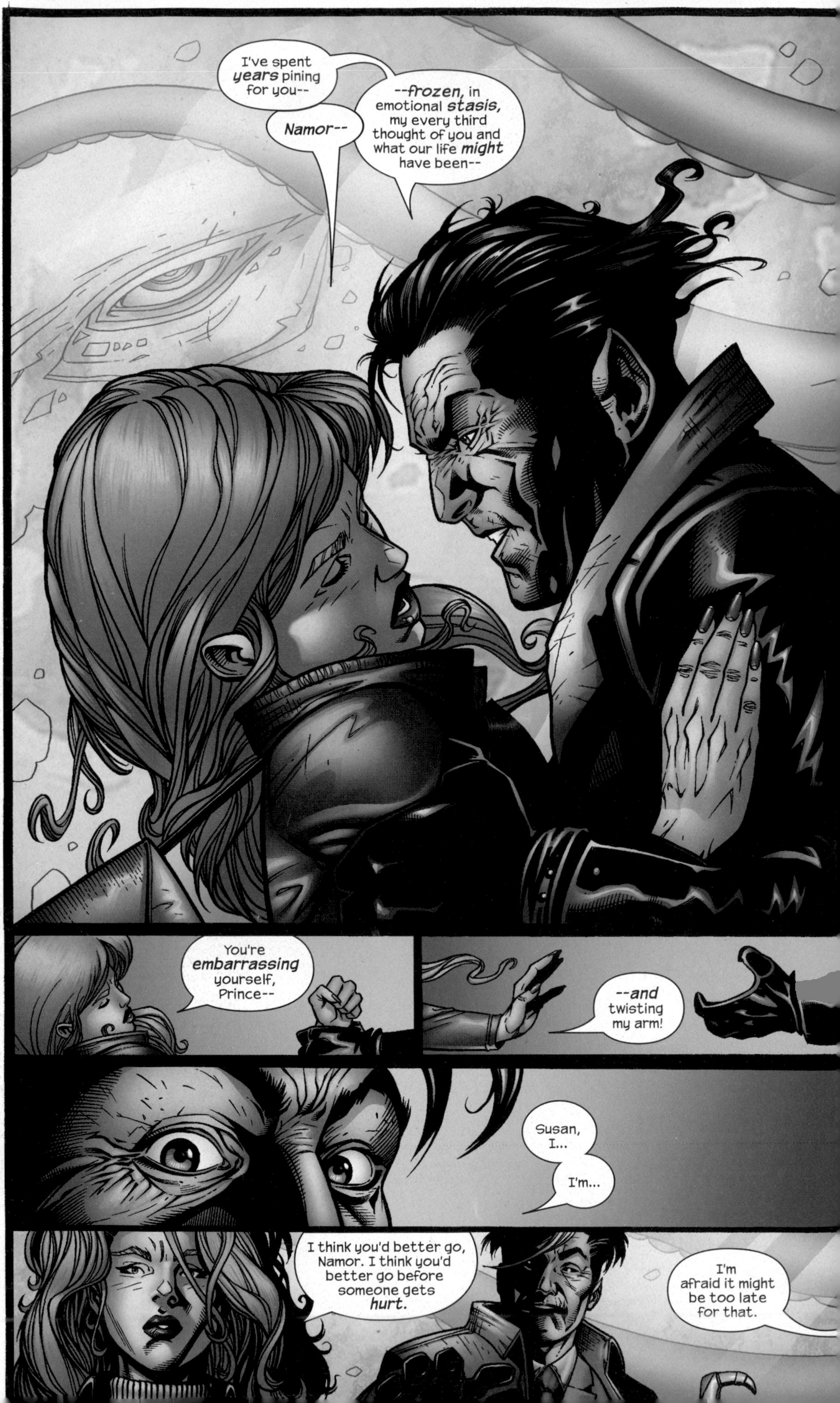
I've spent *years* pining for you--
Namor--
--*frozen,* in emotional *stasis,* my every third thought of you and what our life *might* have been--
You're *embarrassing* yourself, Prince--
--*and* twisting my arm!
Susan, I...
I'm...
I think you'd better go, Namor. I think you'd better go before someone gets *hurt.*
I'm afraid it might be too late for that.

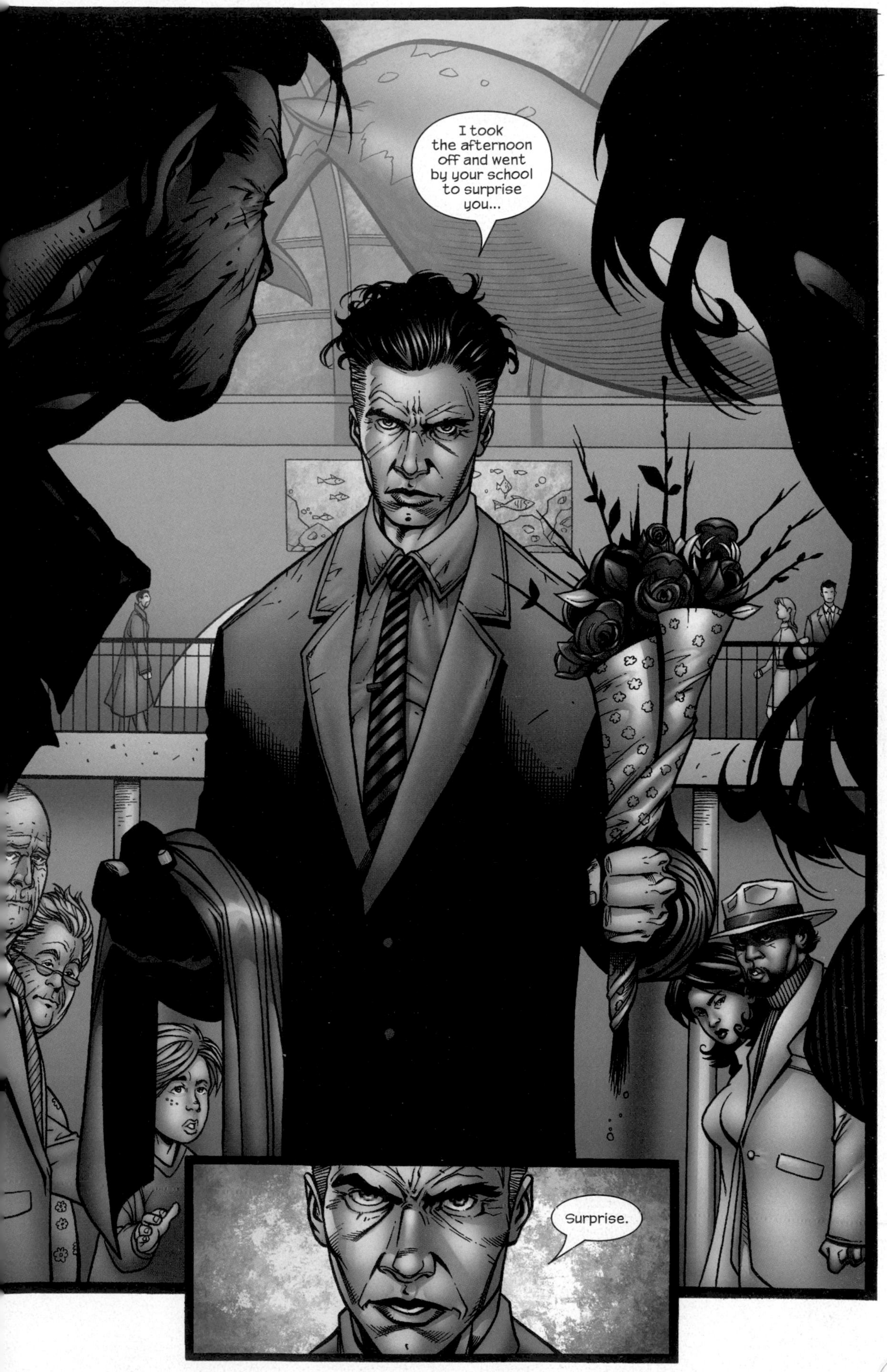
I took the afternoon off and went by your school to surprise you...
Surprise.

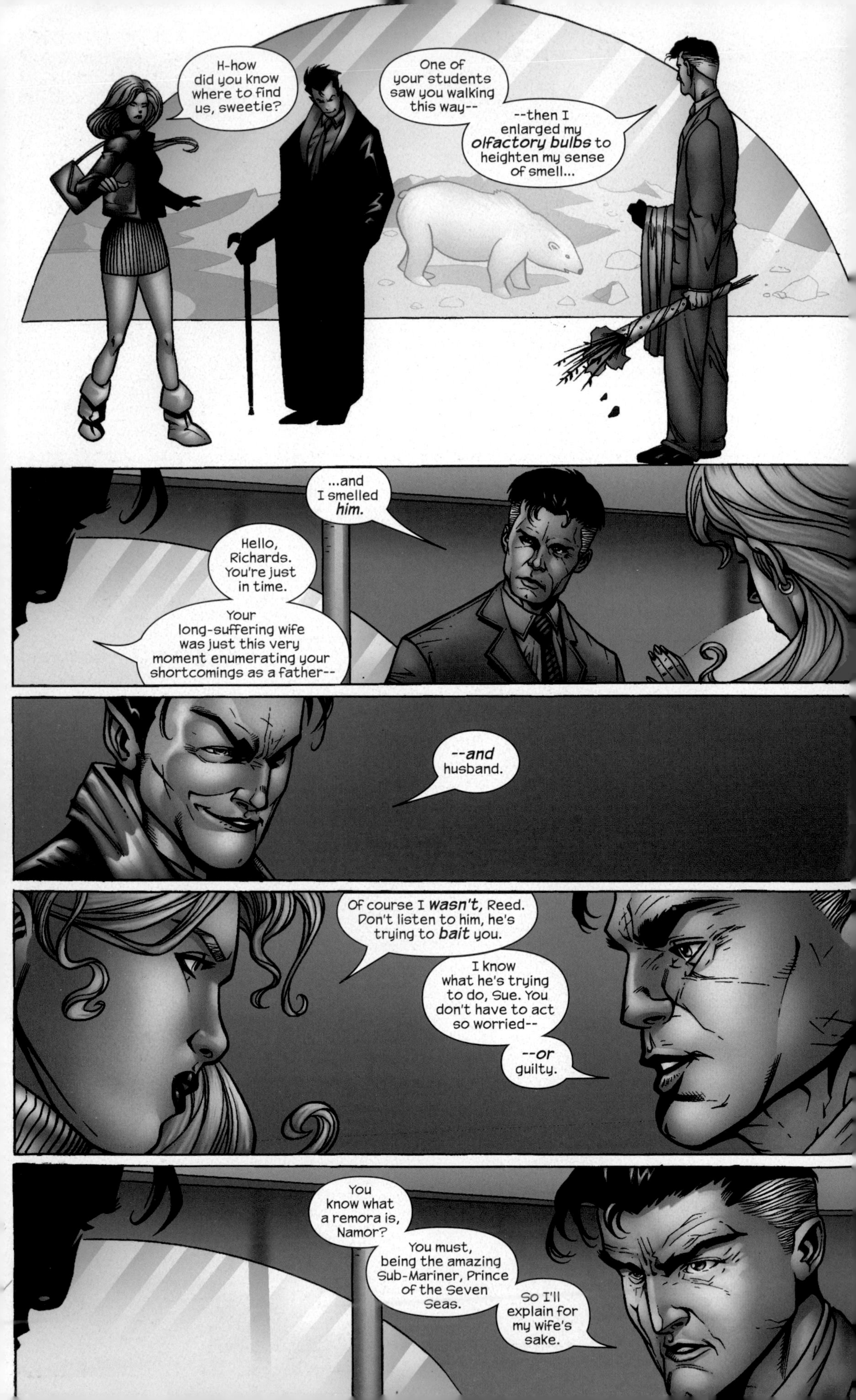
H-how did you know where to find us, sweetie?
One of your students saw you walking this way--
--then I enlarged my *olfactory bulbs* to heighten my sense of smell...
...and I smelled *him.*
Hello, Richards. You're just in time.
Your long-suffering wife was just this very moment enumerating your shortcomings as a father--
--and husband.
Of course I *wasn't,* Reed. Don't listen to him, he's trying to *bait* you.
I know what he's trying to do, Sue. You don't have to act so worried--
--or guilty.
You know what a remora is, Namor?
You must, being the amazing Sub-Mariner, Prince of the Seven Seas.
So I'll explain for my wife's sake.

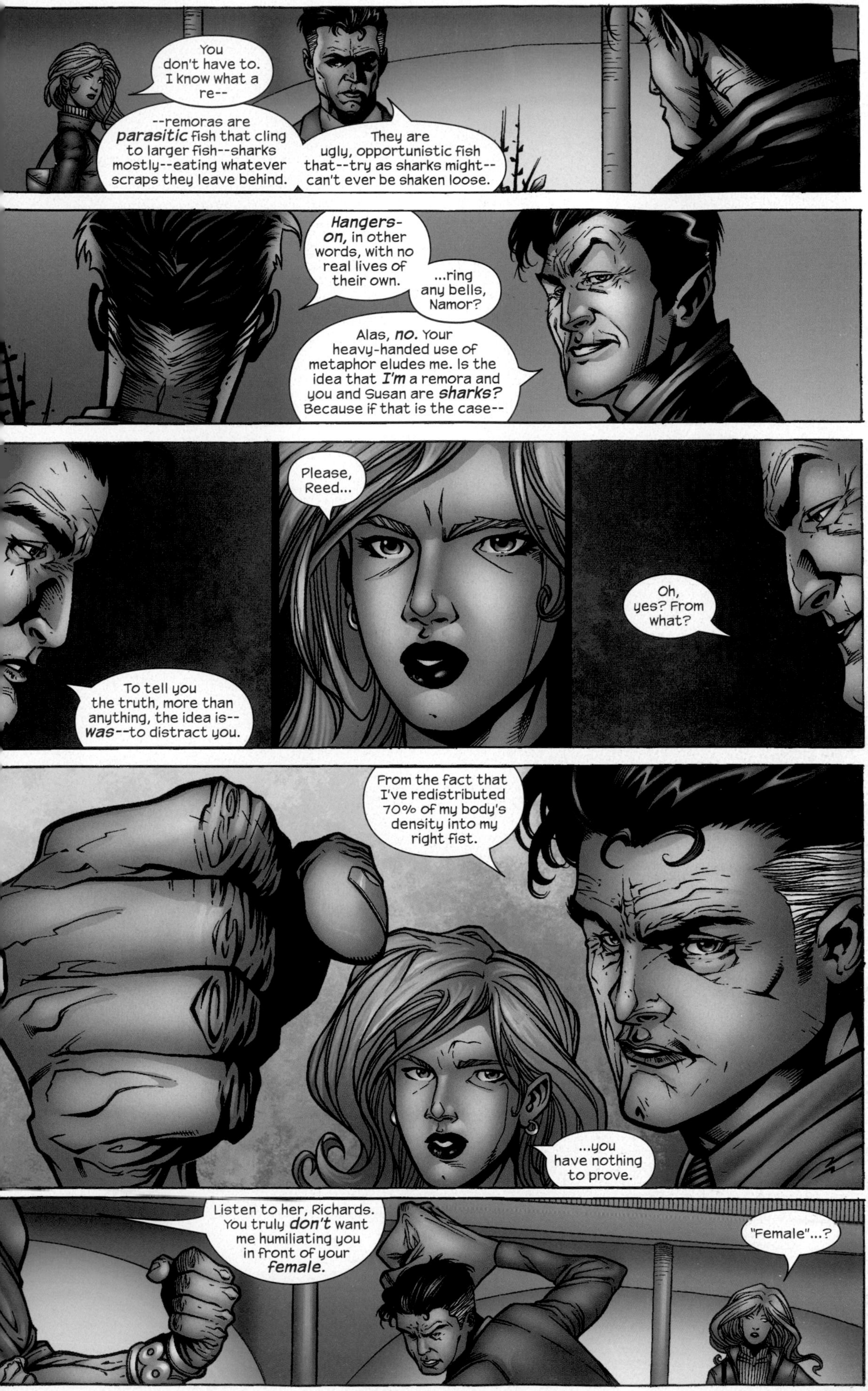
You don't have to. I know what a re--
--remoras are *parasitic* fish that cling to larger fish--sharks mostly--eating whatever scraps they leave behind.
They are ugly, opportunistic fish that--try as sharks might--can't ever be shaken loose.
Hangers-on, in other words, with no real lives of their own.
...ring any bells, Namor?
Alas, *no.* Your heavy-handed use of metaphor eludes me. Is the idea that *I'm* a remora and you and Susan are *sharks?* Because if that is the case--
To tell you the truth, more than anything, the idea is--*was*--to distract you.
Please, Reed...
Oh, yes? From what?
From the fact that I've redistributed 70% of my body's density into my right fist.
...you have nothing to prove.
Listen to her, Richards. You truly *don't* want me humiliating you in front of your *female*.
"Female"...?

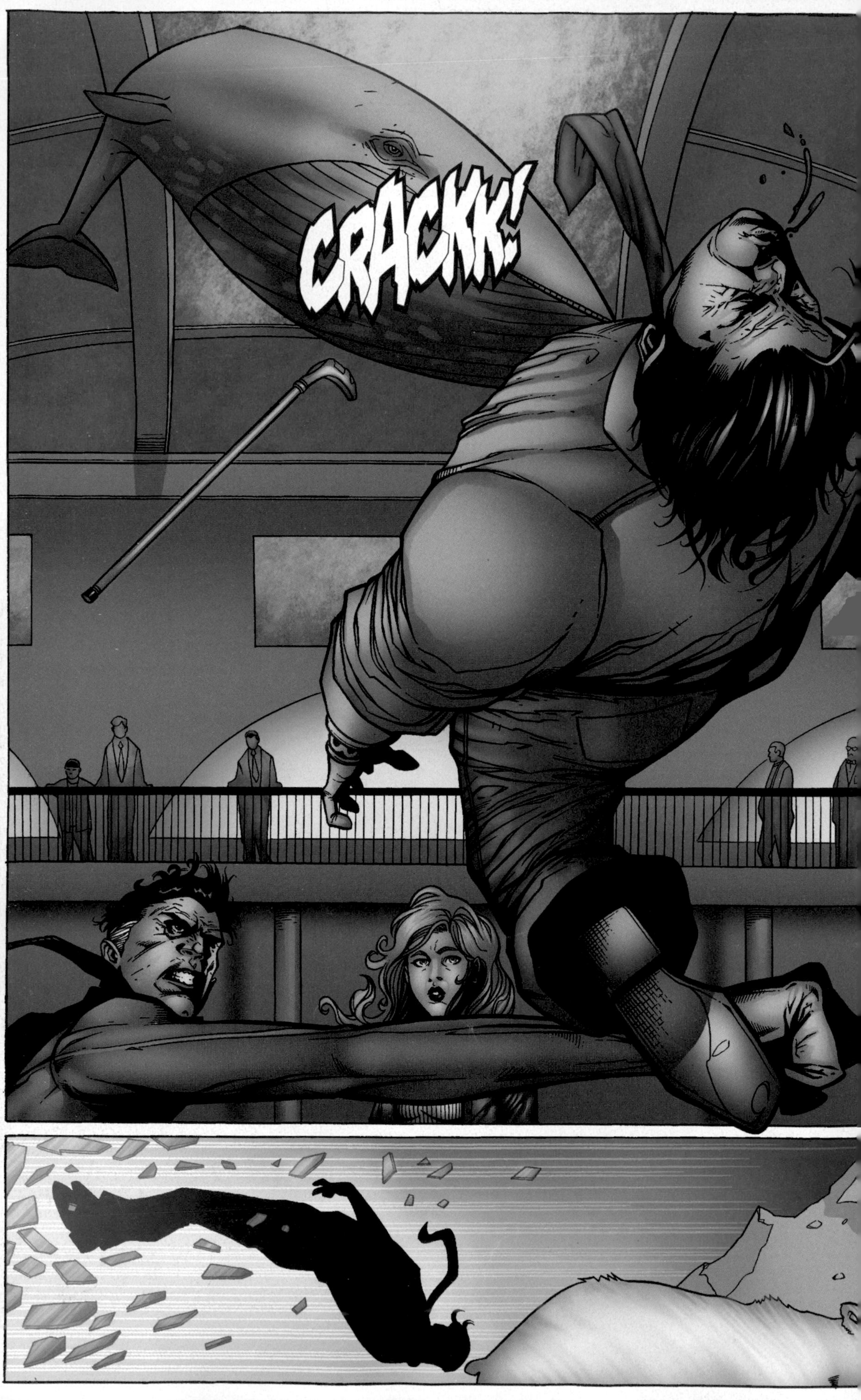
CRACKK!

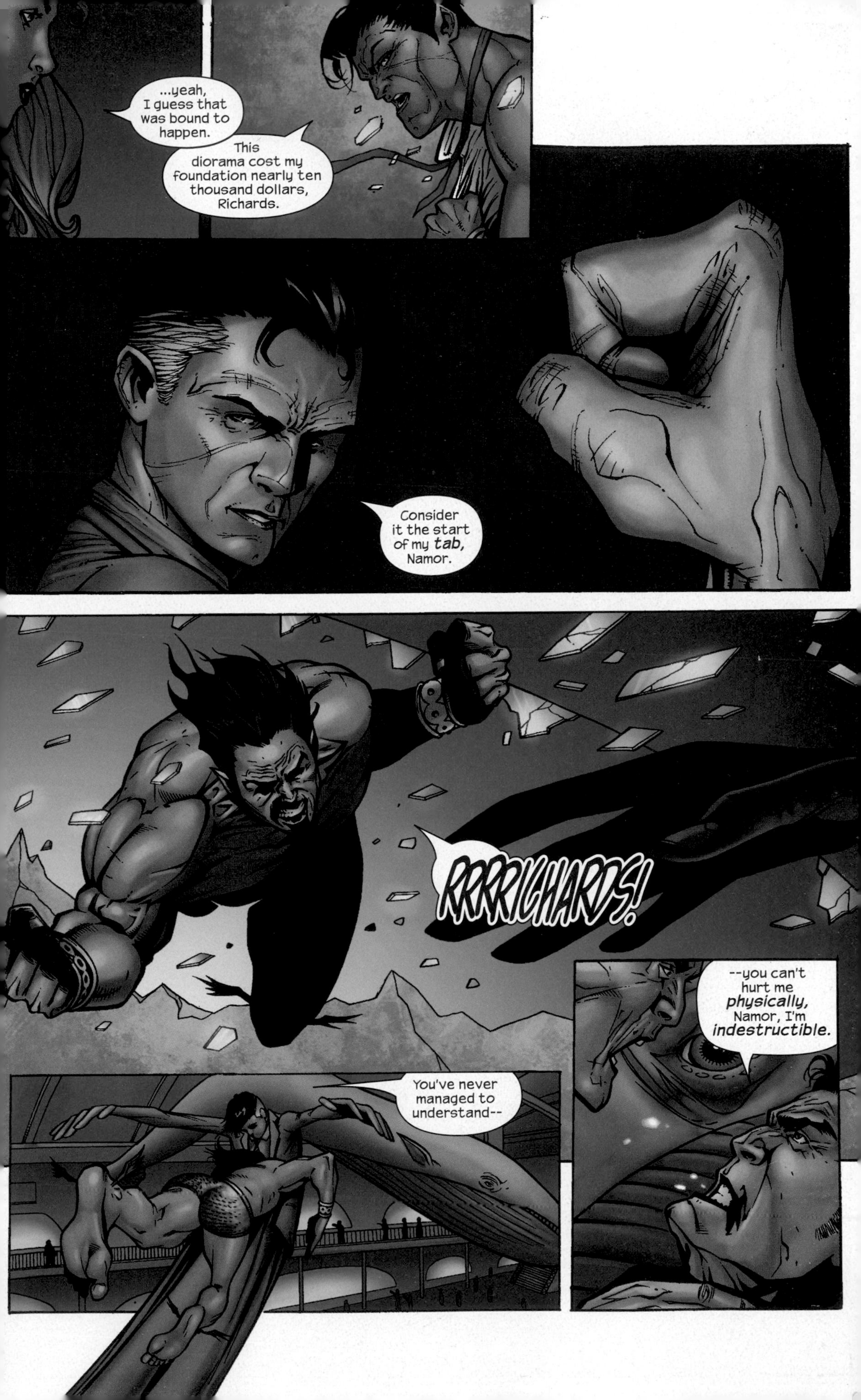
...yeah, I guess that was bound to happen.
This diorama cost my foundation nearly ten thousand dollars, Richards.
Consider it the start of my tab, Namor.
RRRRICHARDS!
You've never managed to understand--
--you can't hurt me physically, Namor, I'm indestructible.

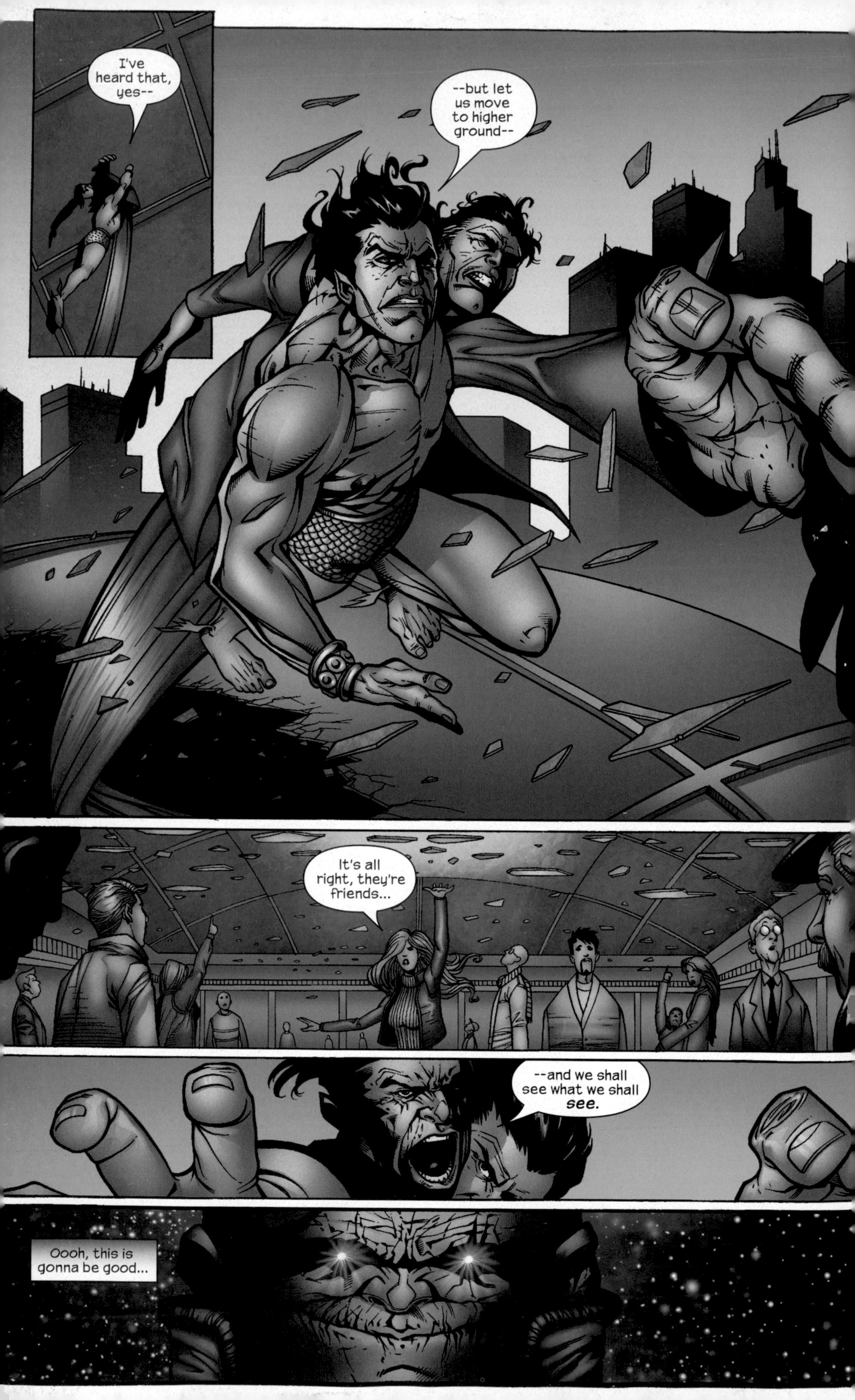
I've heard that, yes--
--but let us move to higher ground--
It's all right, they're friends...
--and we shall see what we shall see.
Oooh, this is gonna be good...

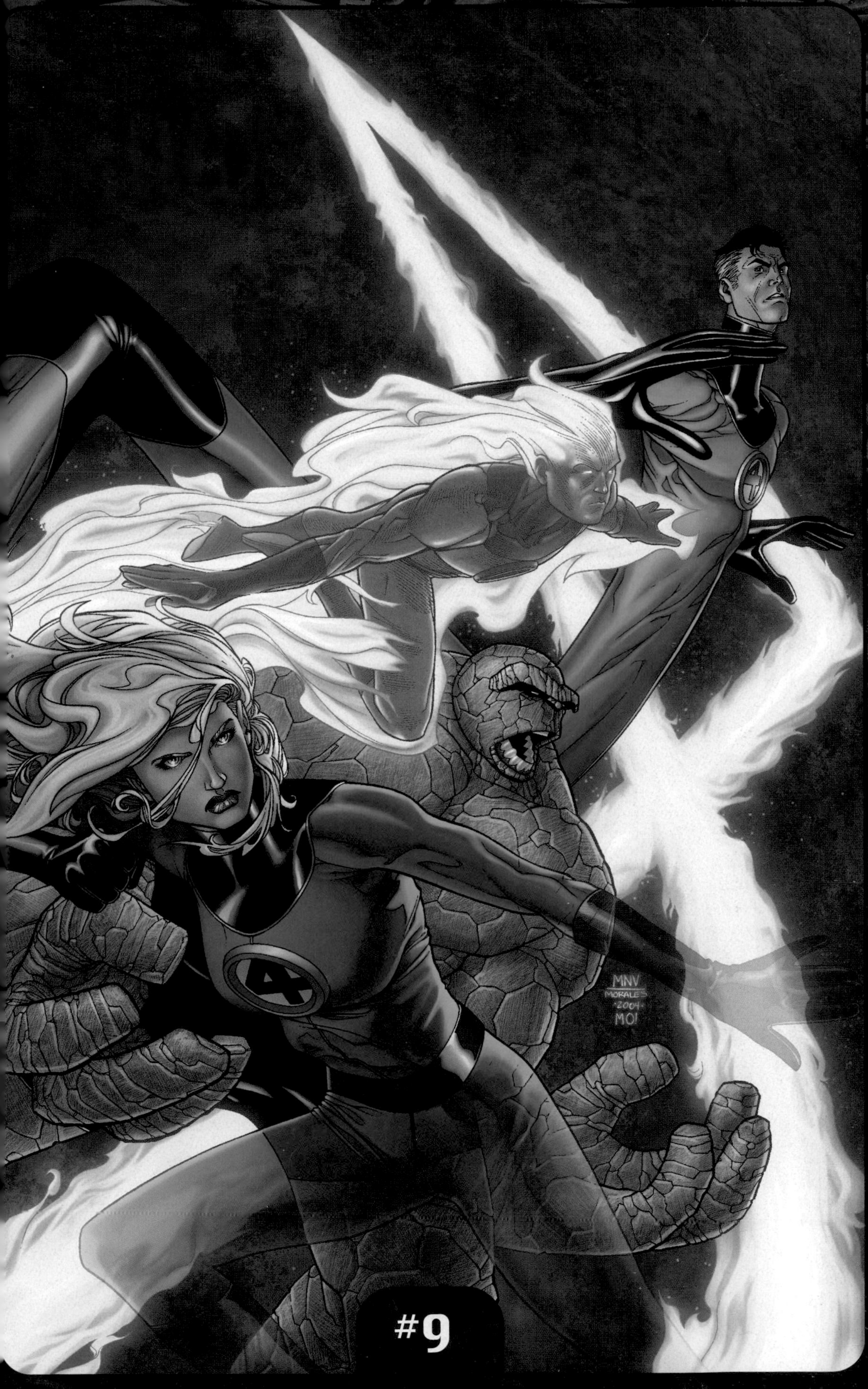
#9

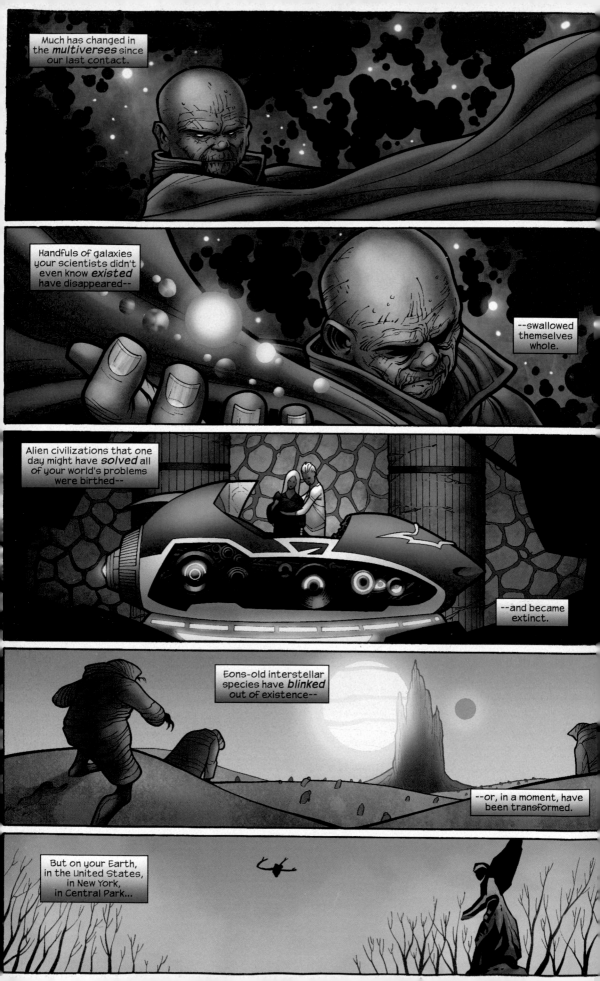

Much has changed in the *multiverses* since our last contact.

Handfuls of galaxies your scientists didn't even know *existed* have disappeared--

--swallowed themselves whole.

Alien civilizations that one day might have *solved* all of your world's problems were birthed--

--and became extinct.

Eons-old interstellar species have *blinked* out of existence--

--or, in a moment, have been transformed.

But on your Earth, in the United States, in New York, in Central Park...

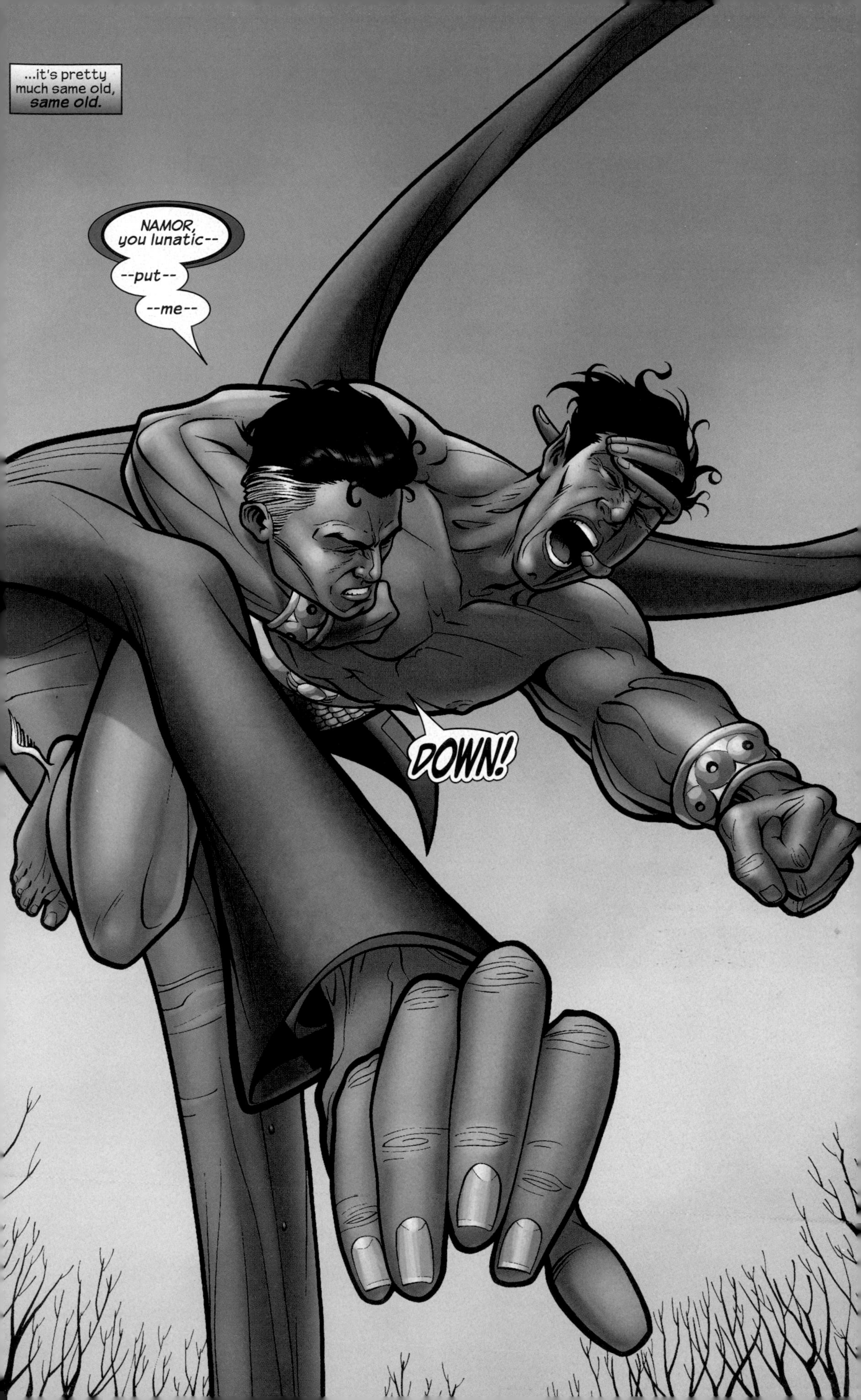
...it's pretty much same old, *same old.*
NAMOR, you lunatic--
--put--
--me--
DOWN!

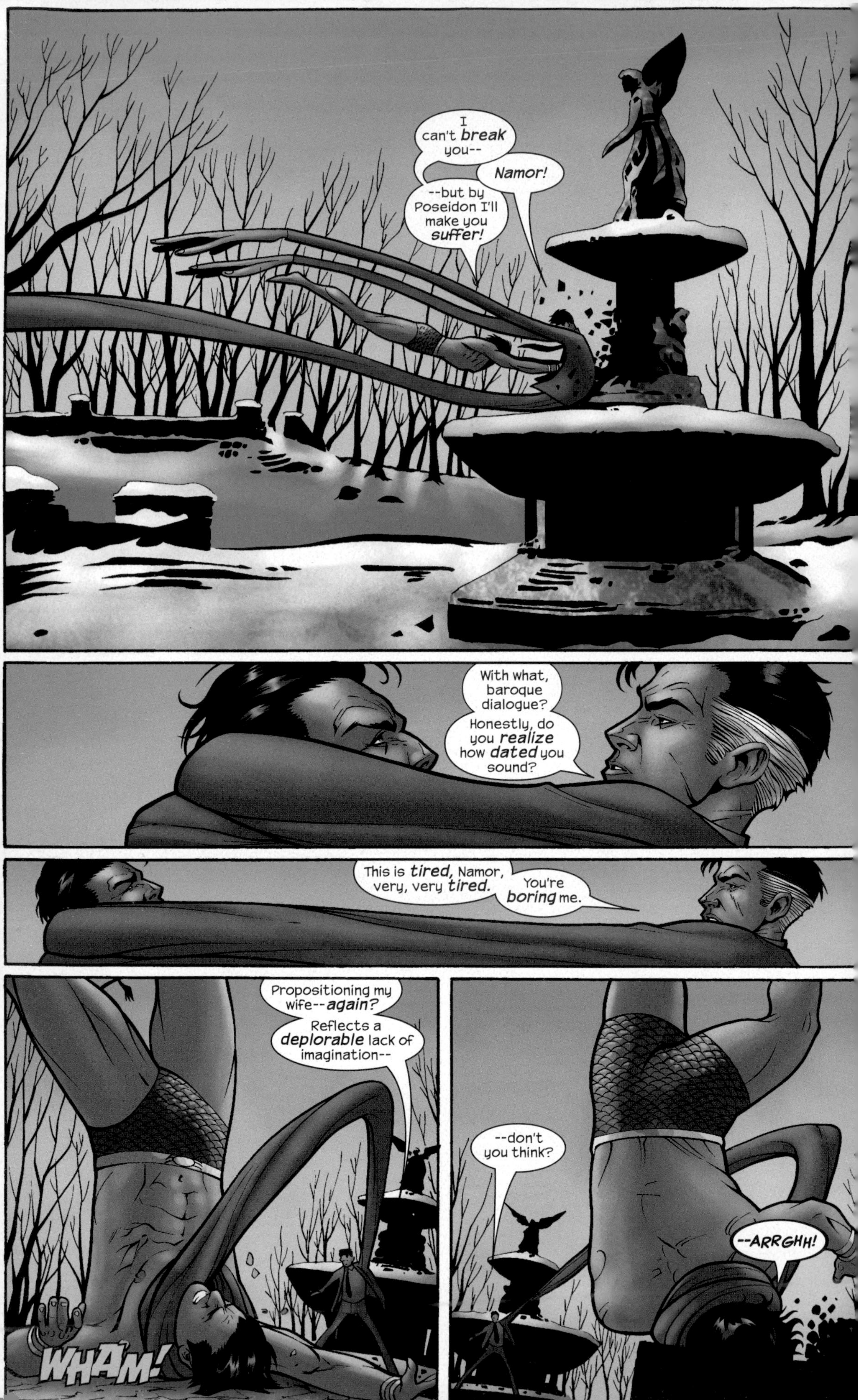

I can't *break* you--
Namor!
--but by Poseidon I'll make you *suffer!*
With what, baroque dialogue?
Honestly, do you *realize* how *dated* you sound?
This is *tired,* Namor, very, very *tired.*
You're *boring* me.
Propositioning my wife--*again?*
Reflects a *deplorable* lack of imagination--
WHAM!
--don't you think?
--ARRGHH!

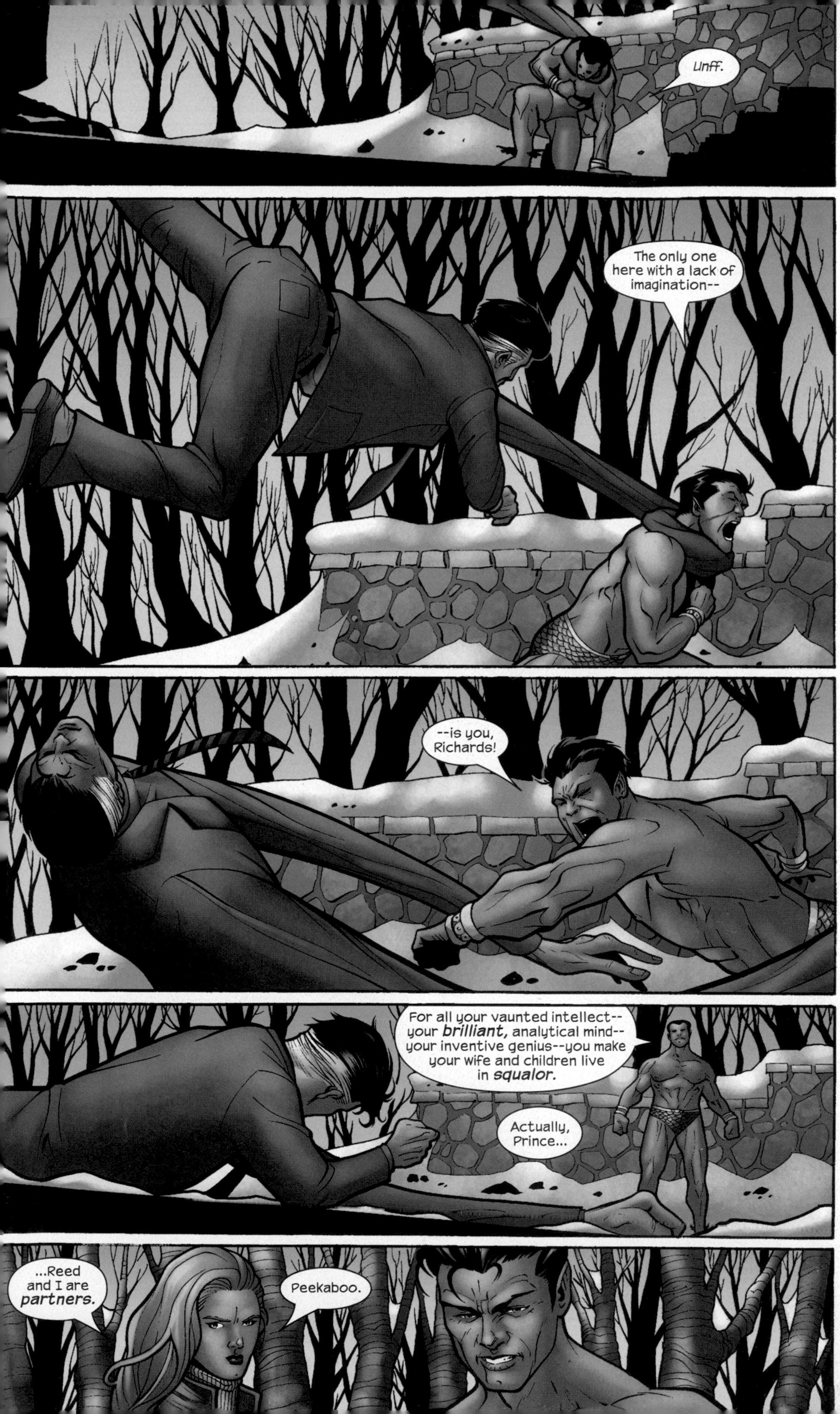
Unff.
The only one here with a lack of imagination--
--is you, Richards!
For all your vaunted intellect--your brilliant, analytical mind--your inventive genius--you make your wife and children live in squalor.
Actually, Prince...
...Reed and I are partners.
Peekaboo.

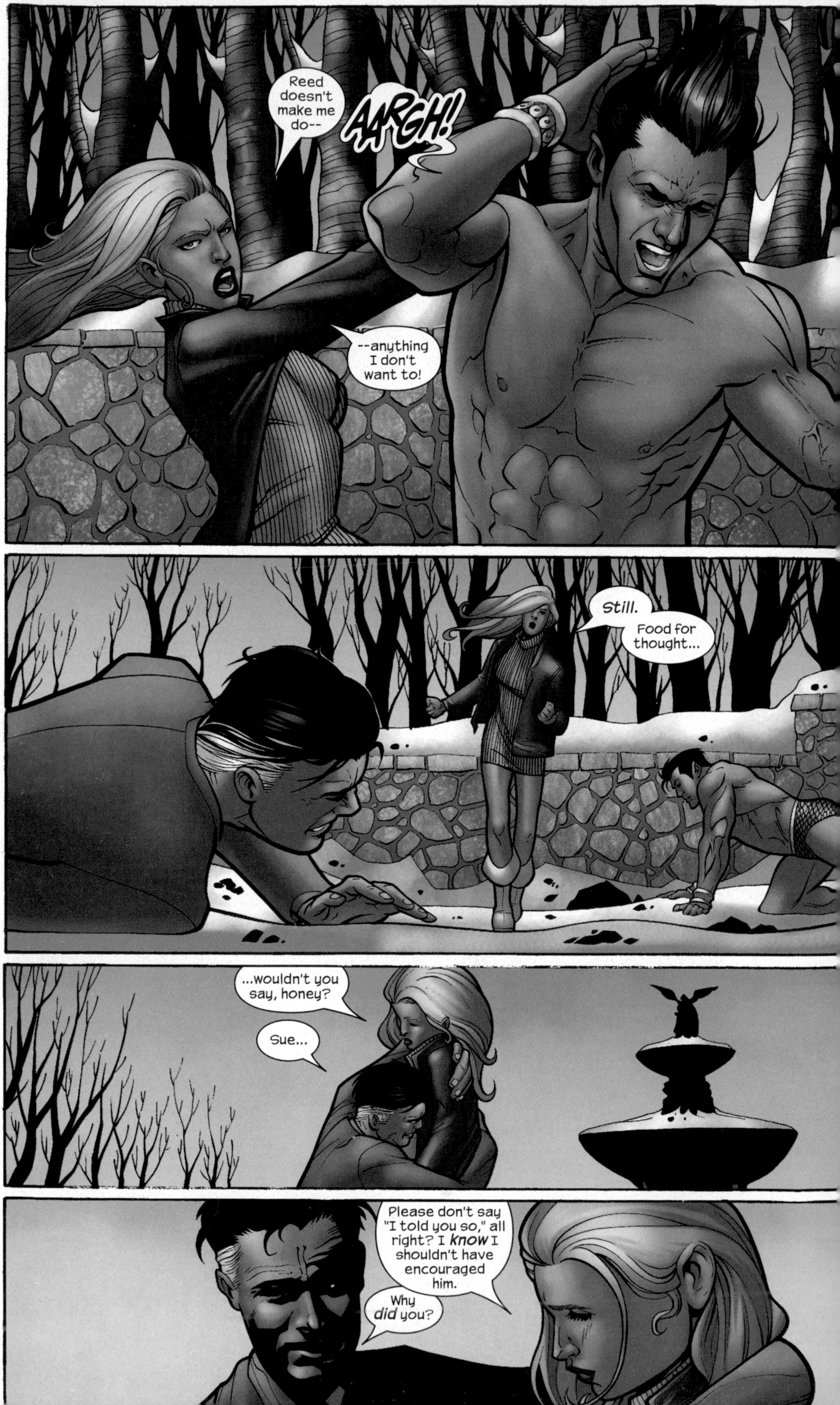
Reed doesn't make me do--
AARGH!
--anything I don't want to!
Still.
Food for thought...
...wouldn't you say, honey?
Sue...
Please don't say "I told you so," all right? I *know* I shouldn't have encouraged him.
Why *did* you?

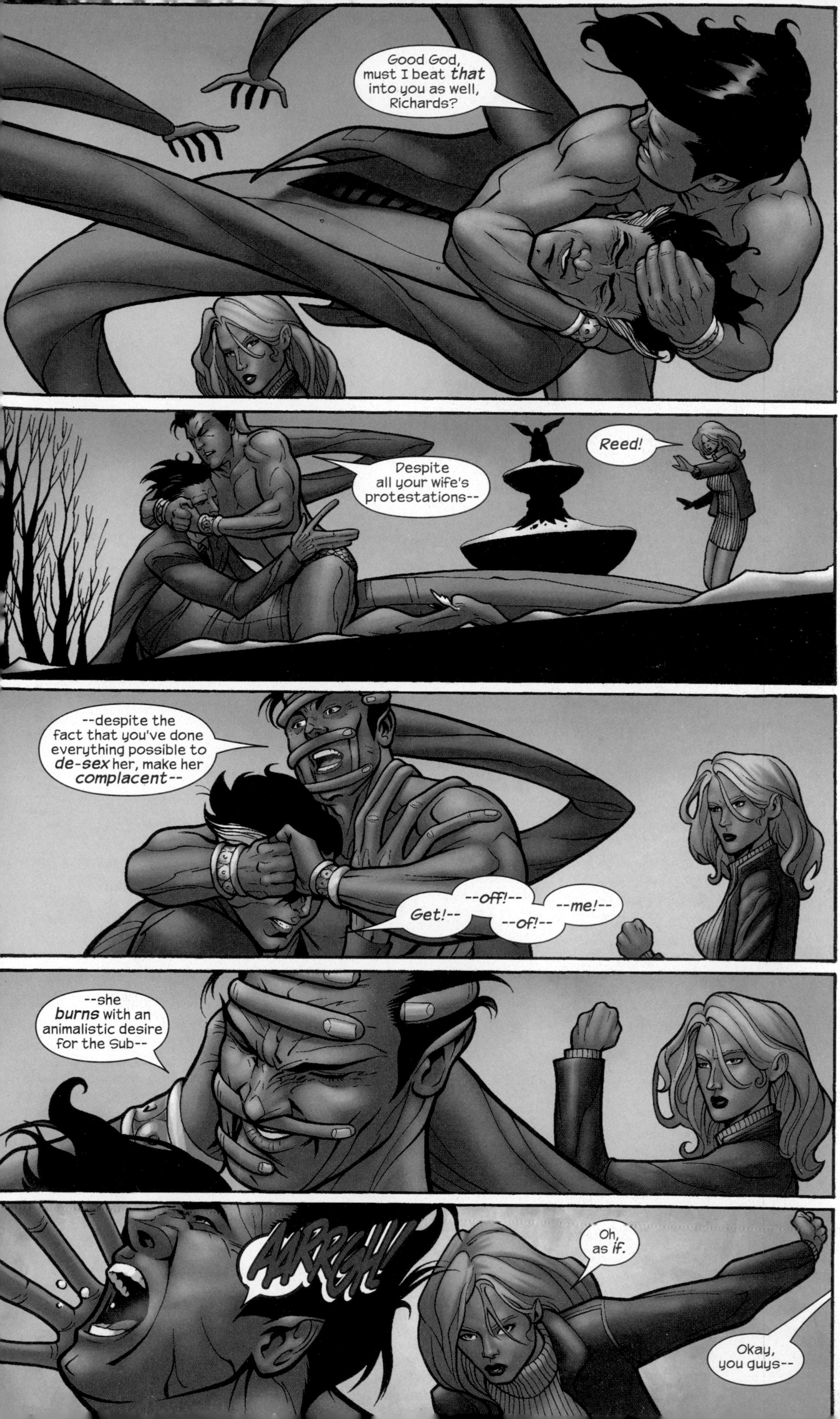

Good God, must I beat *that* into you as well, Richards?
Despite all your wife's protestations--
Reed!
--despite the fact that you've done everything possible to ***de-sex*** her, make her ***complacent***--
Get!--
--off!--
--of!--
--me!--
--she ***burns*** with an animalistic desire for the Sub--
AARRGH!
Oh, as *if.*
Okay, you guys--

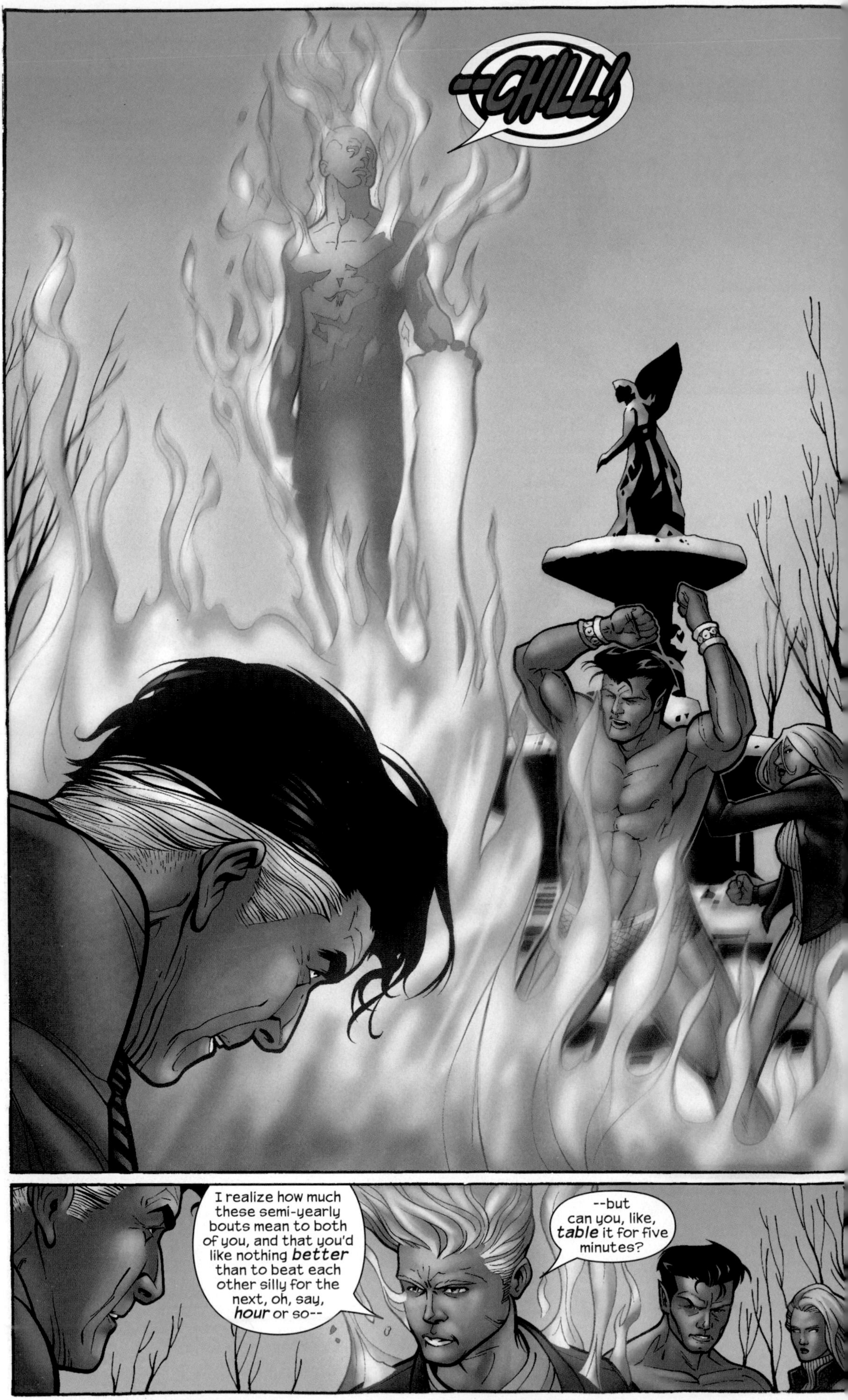
--CHILL!
I realize how much these semi-yearly bouts mean to both of you, and that you'd like nothing better than to beat each other silly for the next, oh, say, hour or so--
--but can you, like, table it for five minutes?

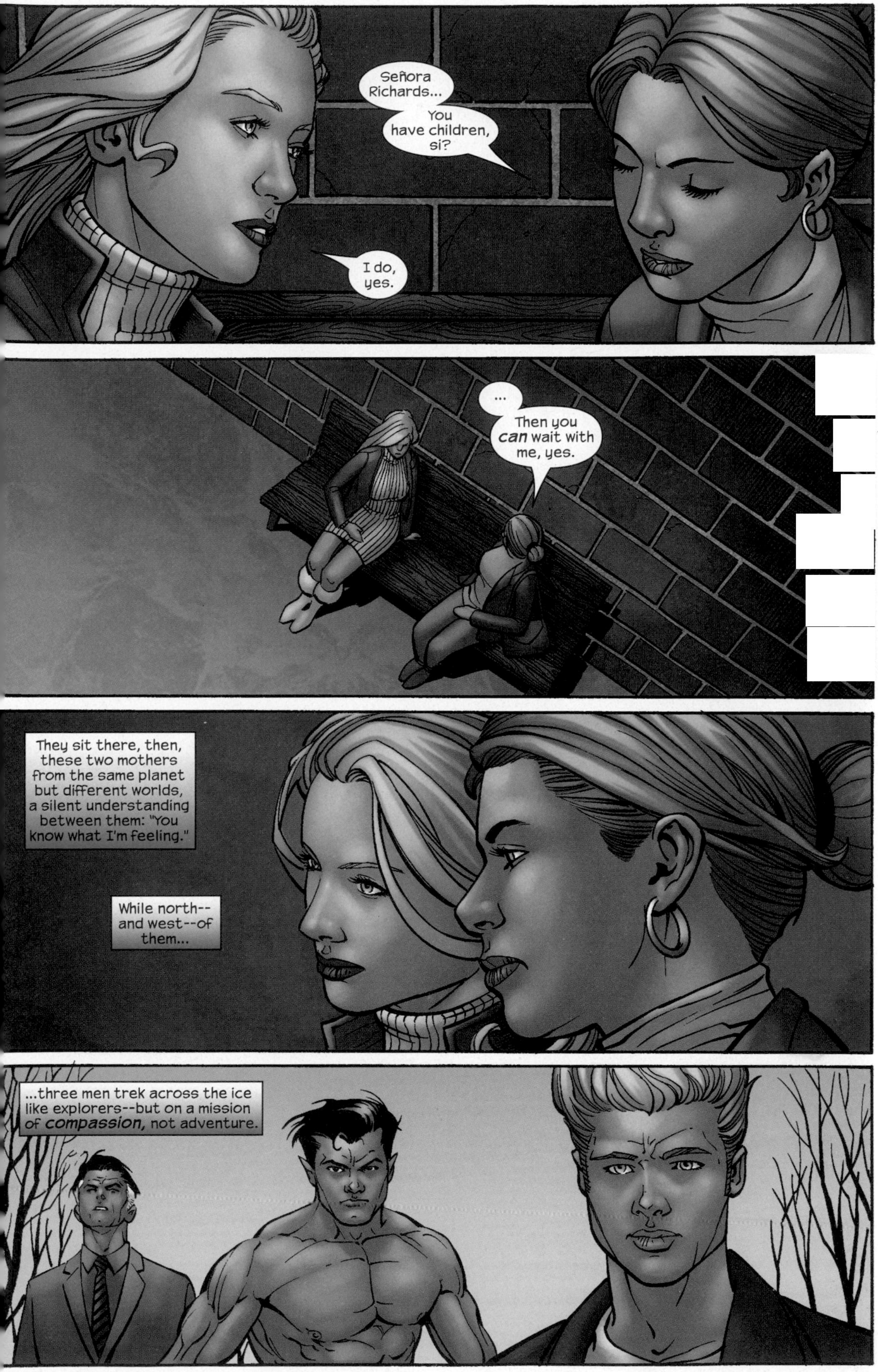
Señora Richards...
You have children, si?
I do, yes.
...
Then you *can* wait with me, yes.
They sit there, then, these two mothers from the same planet but different worlds, a silent understanding between them: "You know what I'm feeling."
While north--and west--of them...
...three men trek across the ice like explorers--but on a mission of *compassion,* not adventure.

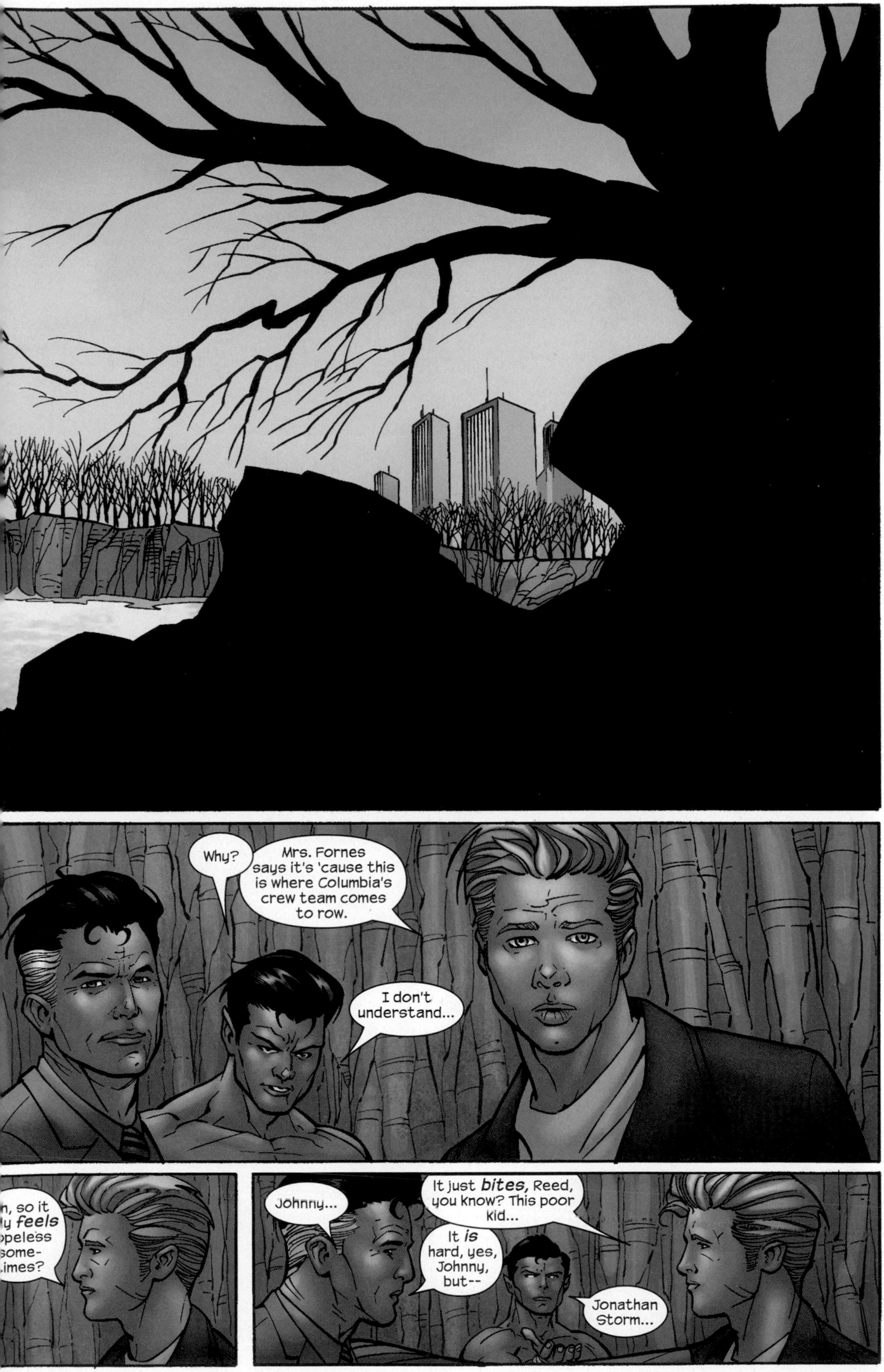
Why?
Mrs. Fornes says it's 'cause this is where Columbia's crew team comes to row.
I don't understand...
n, so it y *feels* opeless some- imes?
Johnny...
It just *bites,* Reed, you know? This poor kid...
It *is* hard, yes, Johnny, but--
Jonathan Storm...

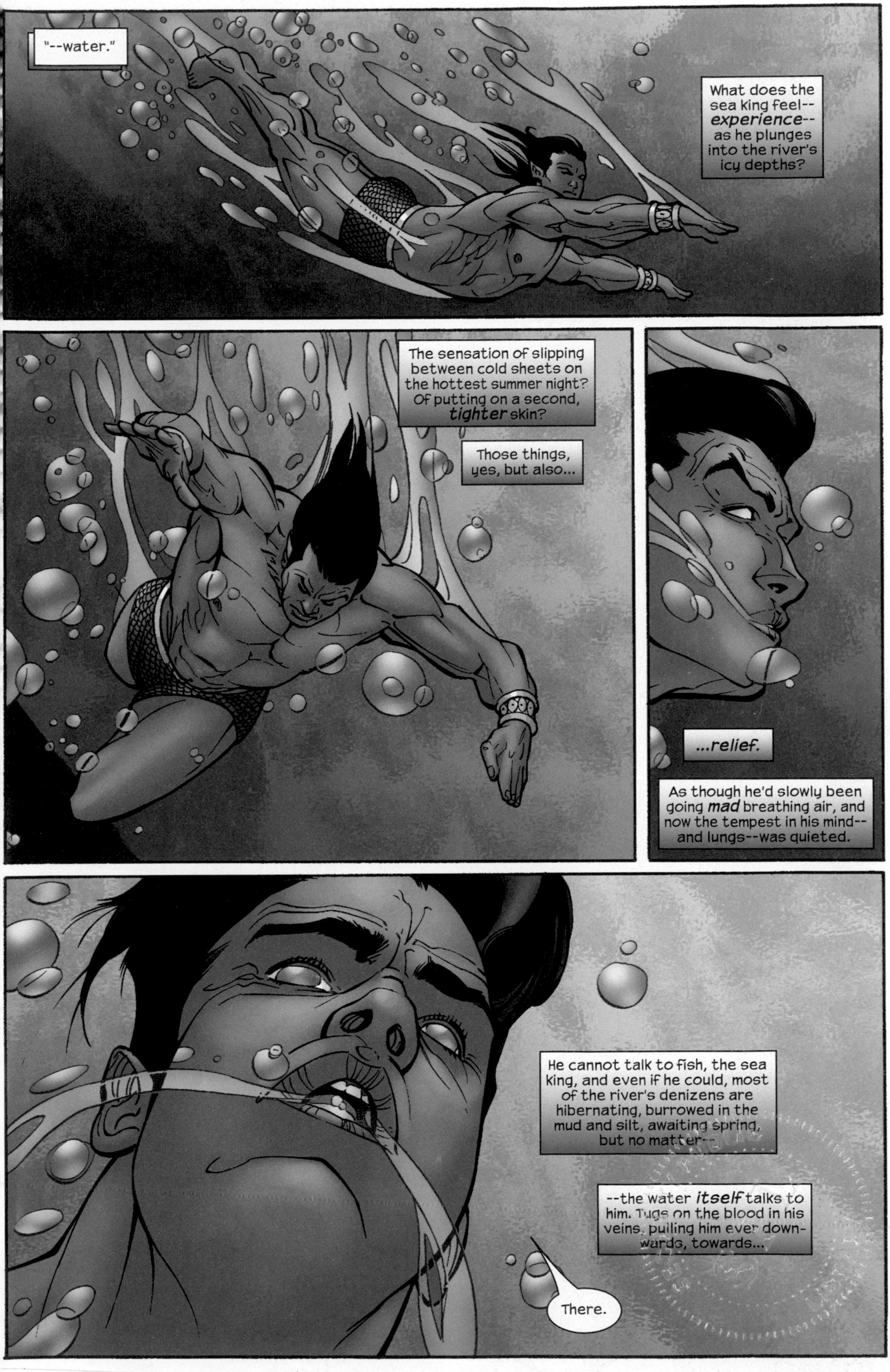
"--water."
What does the sea king feel-- experience-- as he plunges into the river's icy depths?
The sensation of slipping between cold sheets on the hottest summer night? Of putting on a second, tighter skin?
Those things, yes, but also...
...relief.
As though he'd slowly been going mad breathing air, and now the tempest in his mind--and lungs--was quieted.
He cannot talk to fish, the sea king, and even if he could, most of the river's denizens are hibernating, burrowed in the mud and silt, awaiting spring, but no matter--
--the water itself talks to him. Tugs on the blood in his veins, pulling him ever downwards, towards...
There.

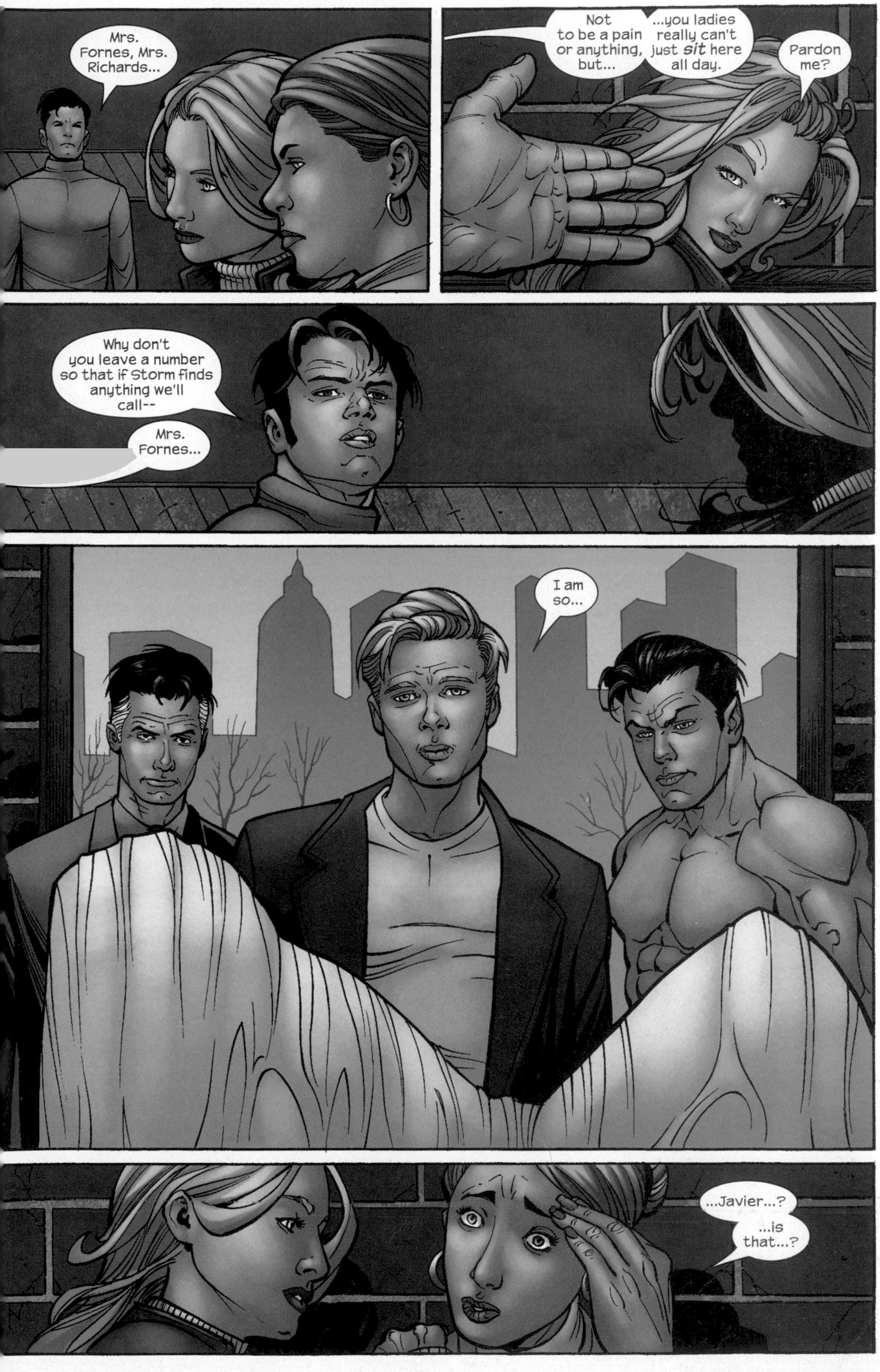
Mrs. Fornes, Mrs. Richards...
Not to be a pain or anything, but...
...you ladies really can't just *sit* here all day.
Pardon me?
Why don't you leave a number so that if Storm finds anything we'll call--
Mrs. Fornes...
I am so...
...Javier...?
...is that...?

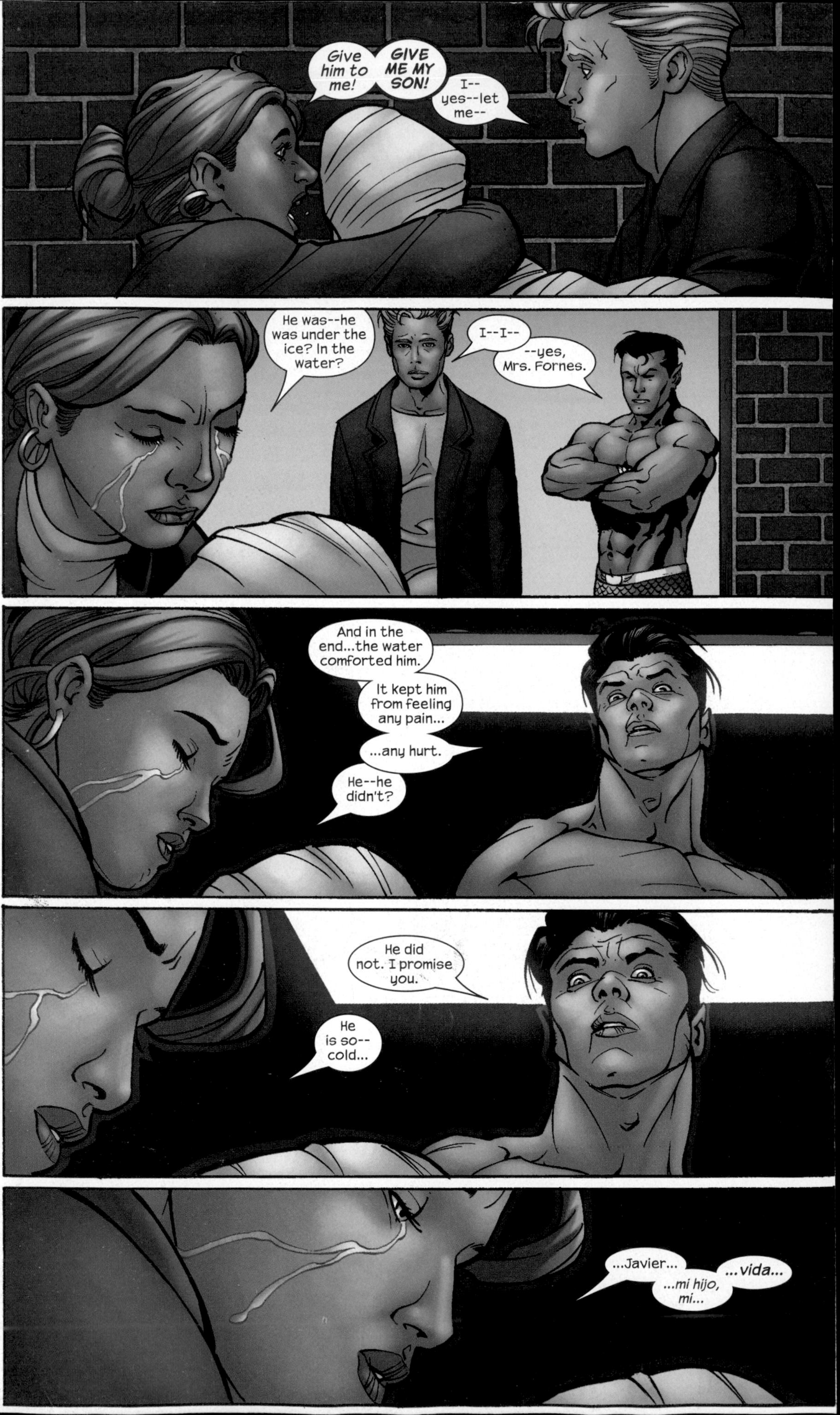
Give him to me!
GIVE ME MY SON!
I-- yes--let me--
He was--he was under the ice? In the water?
I--I--
--yes, Mrs. Fornes.
And in the end...the water comforted him.
It kept him from feeling any pain...
...any hurt.
He--he didn't?
He did not. I promise you.
He is so-- cold...
...Javier...
...mi hijo, mi...
...vida...

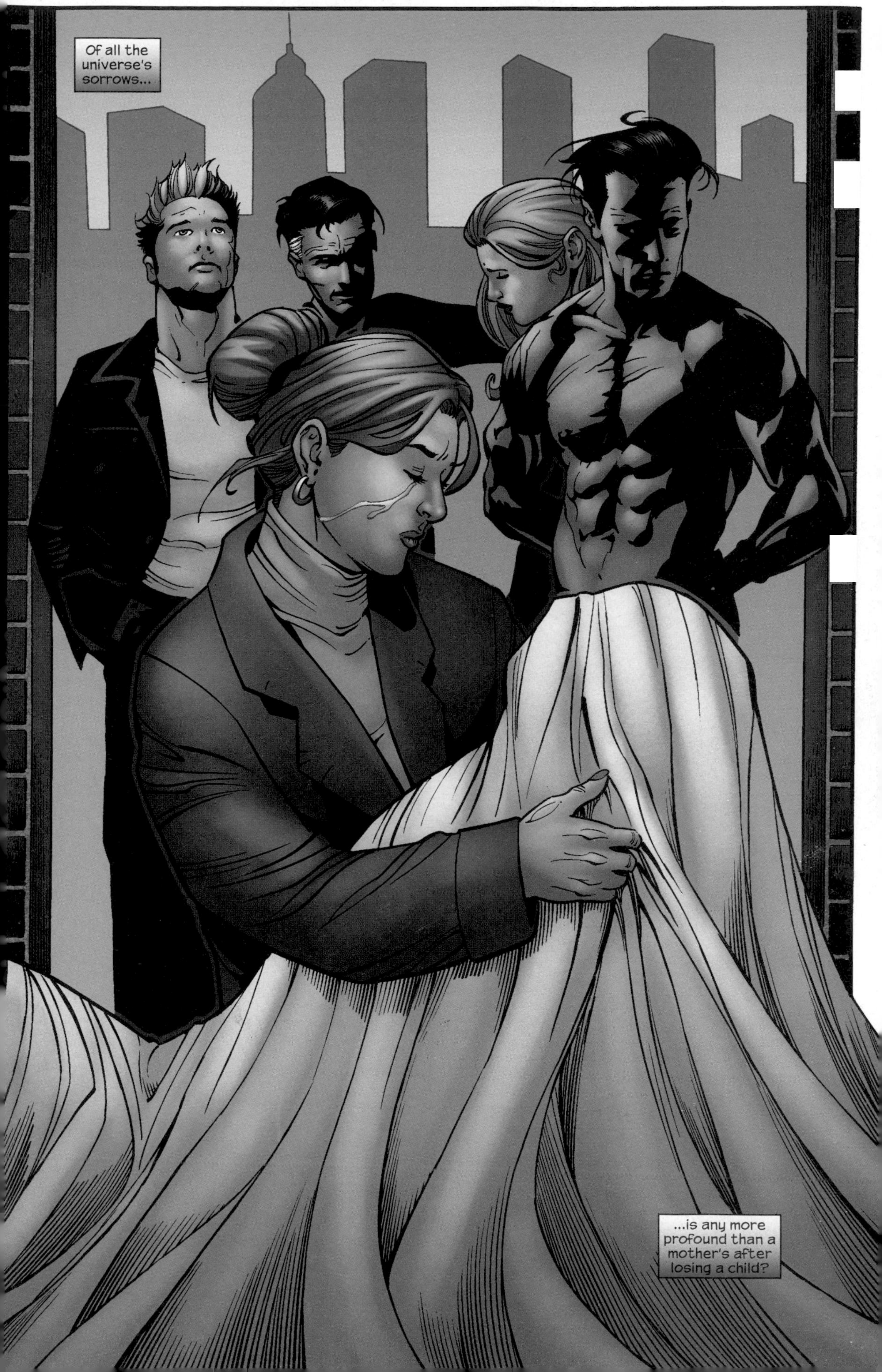
Of all the universe's sorrows...
...is any more profound than a mother's after losing a child?

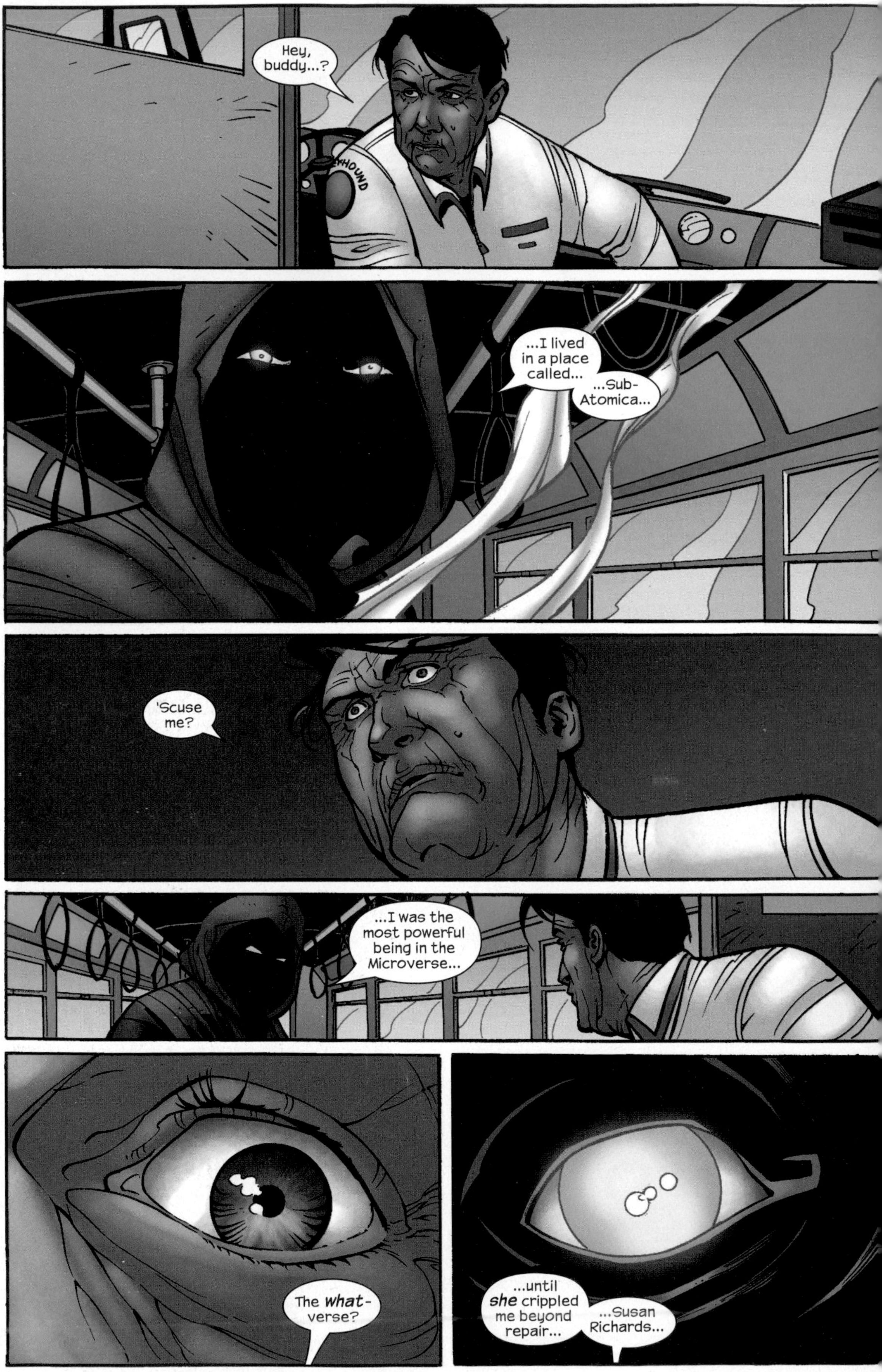
Hey, buddy...?
...I lived in a place called...
...Sub-Atomica...
'Scuse me?
...I was the most powerful being in the Microverse...
The *what*-verse?
...until *she* crippled me beyond repair...
...Susan Richards...

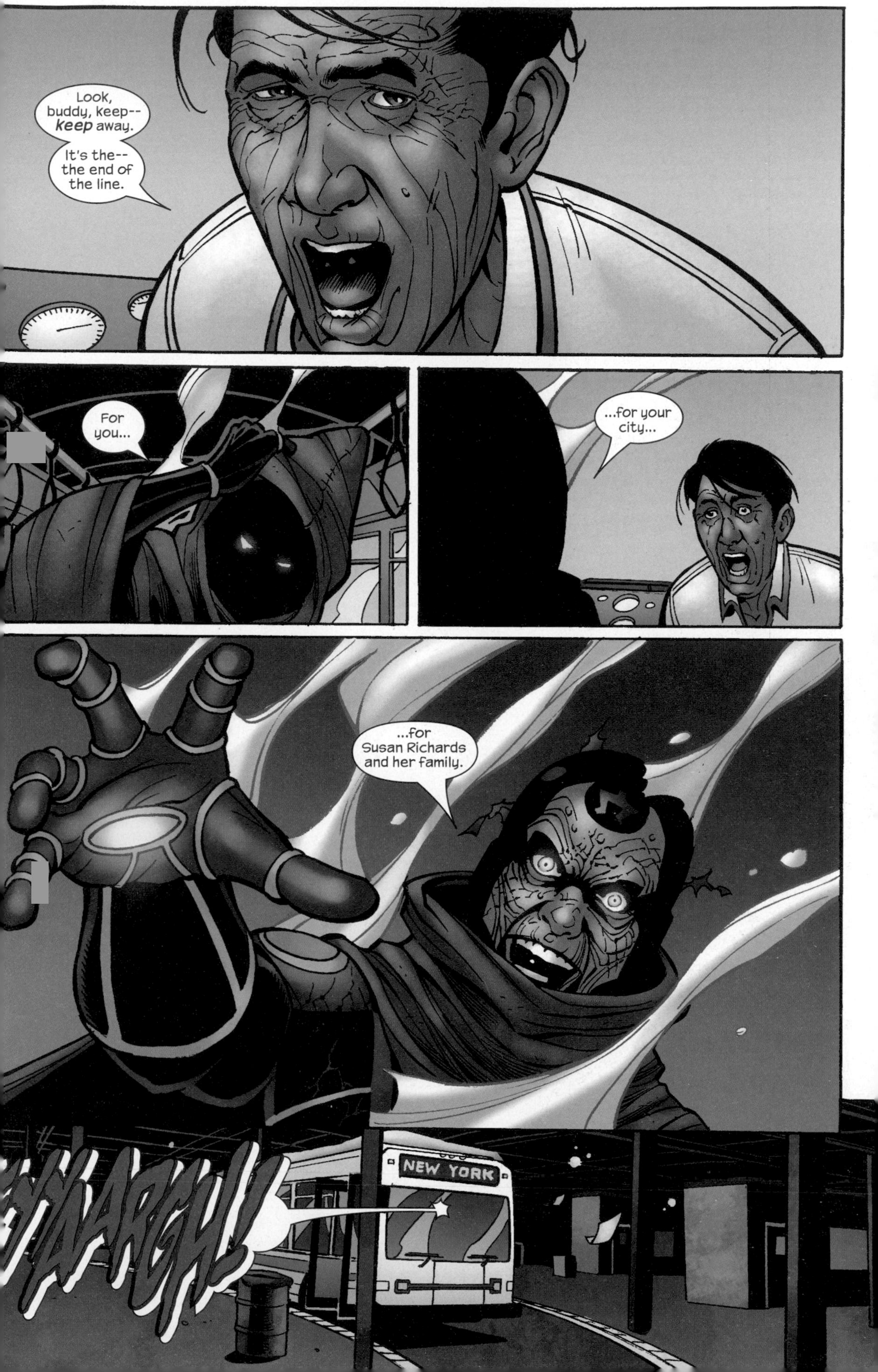
Look, buddy, keep-- *keep* away.
It's the-- the end of the line.
For you...
...for your city...
...for Susan Richards and her family.
NEW YORK

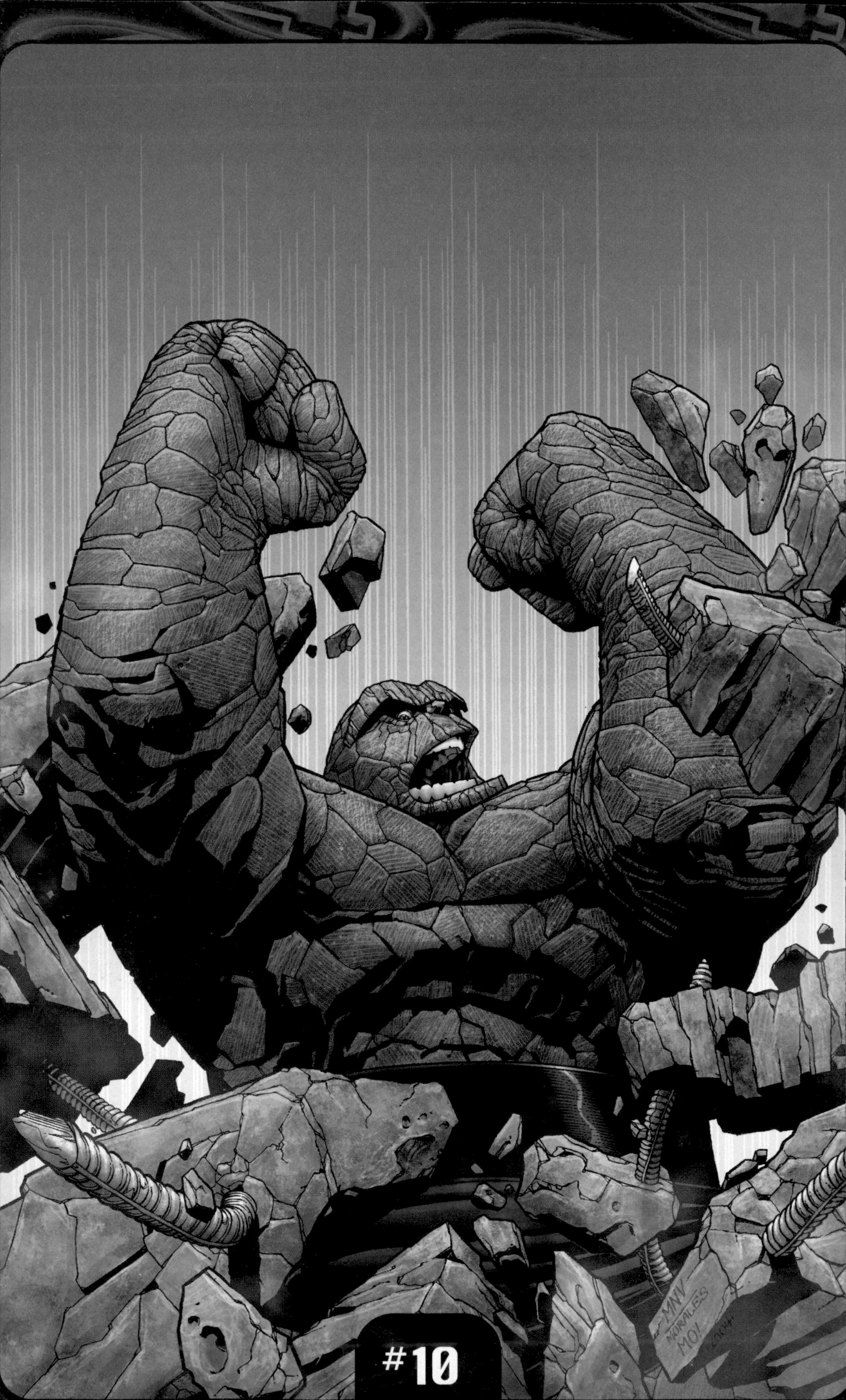
#10

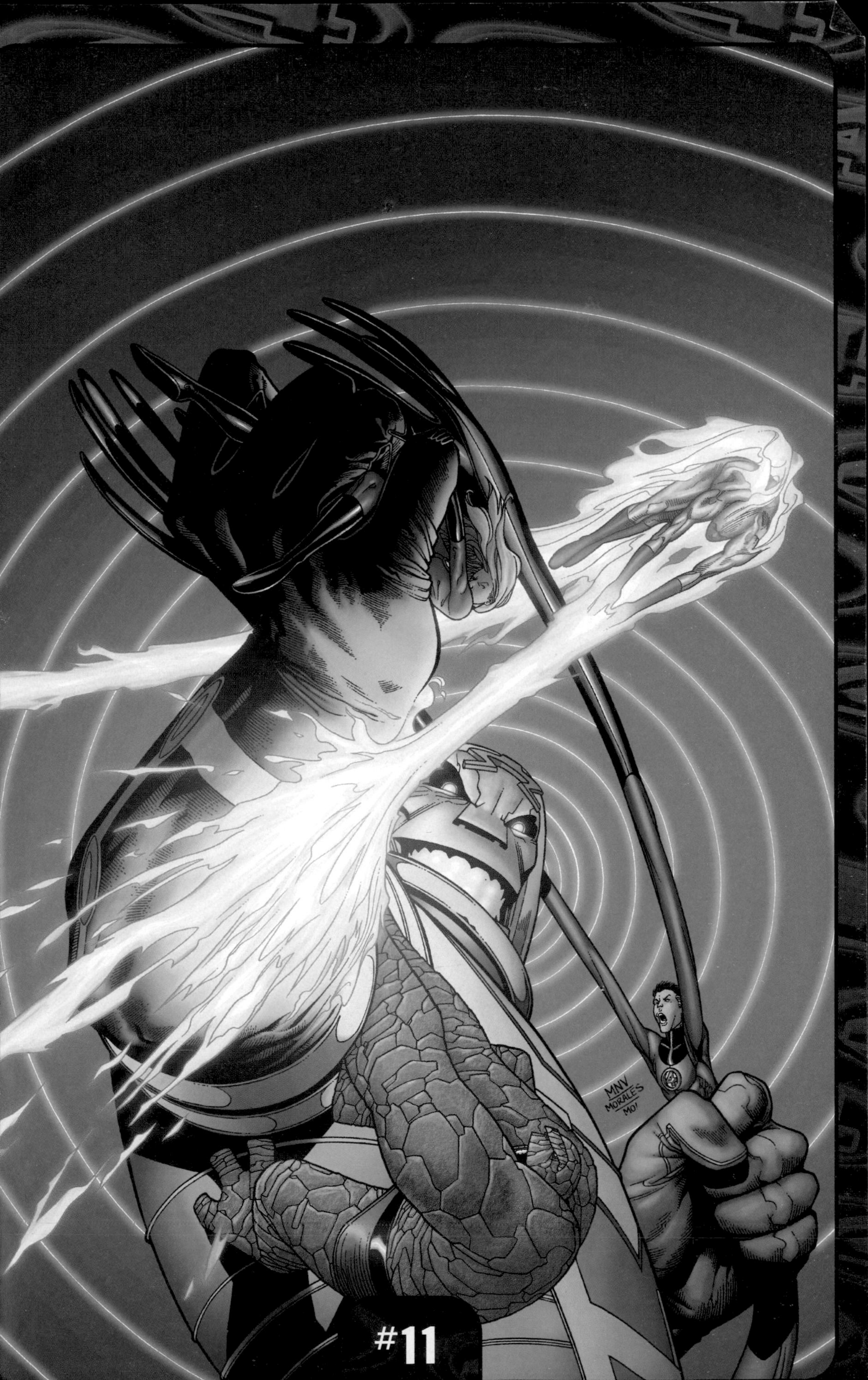
MNV
MORALES
MO!
#11

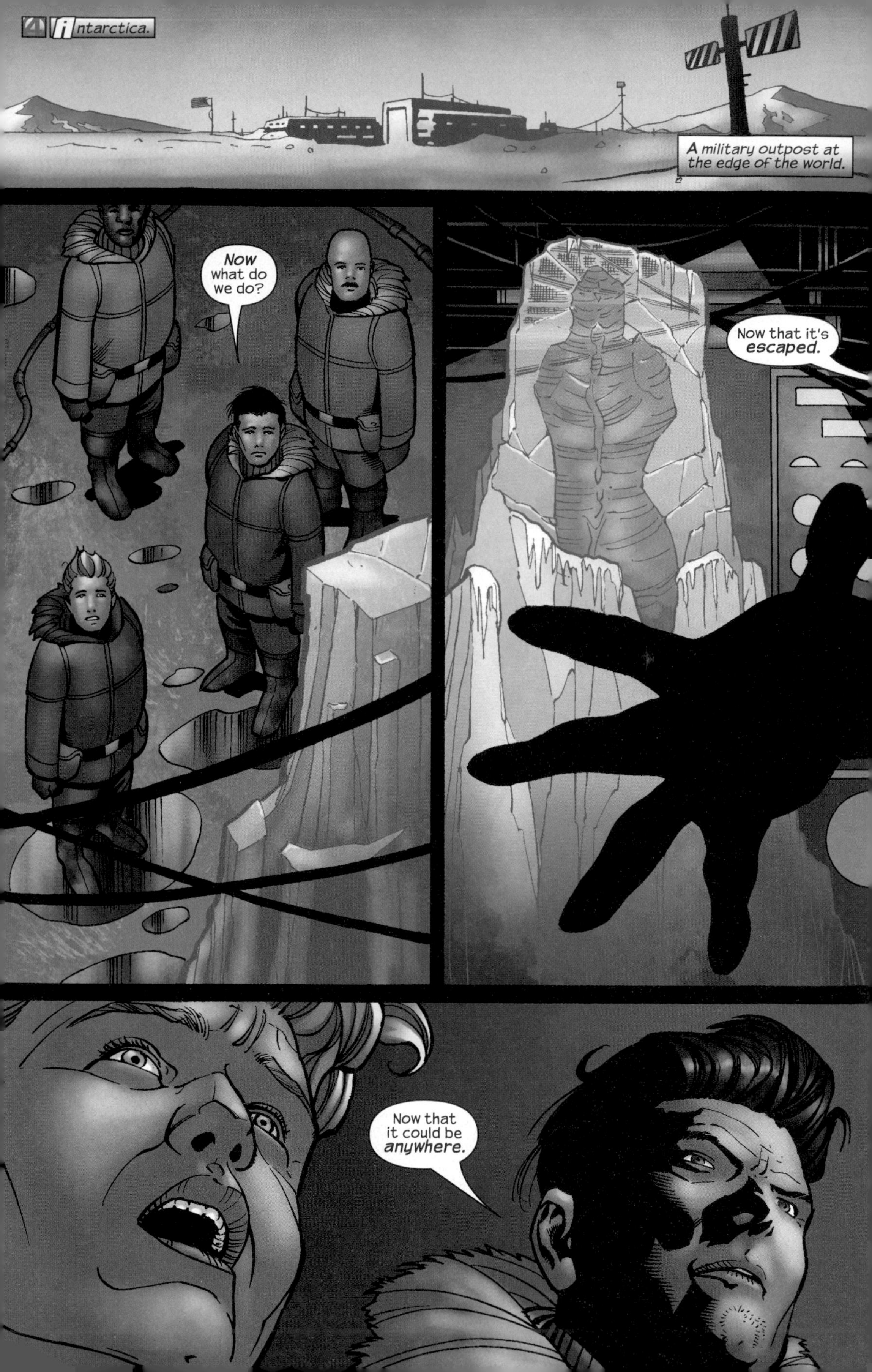
Antarctica.
A military outpost at the edge of the world.
Now what do we do?
Now that it's escaped.
Now that it could be anywhere.

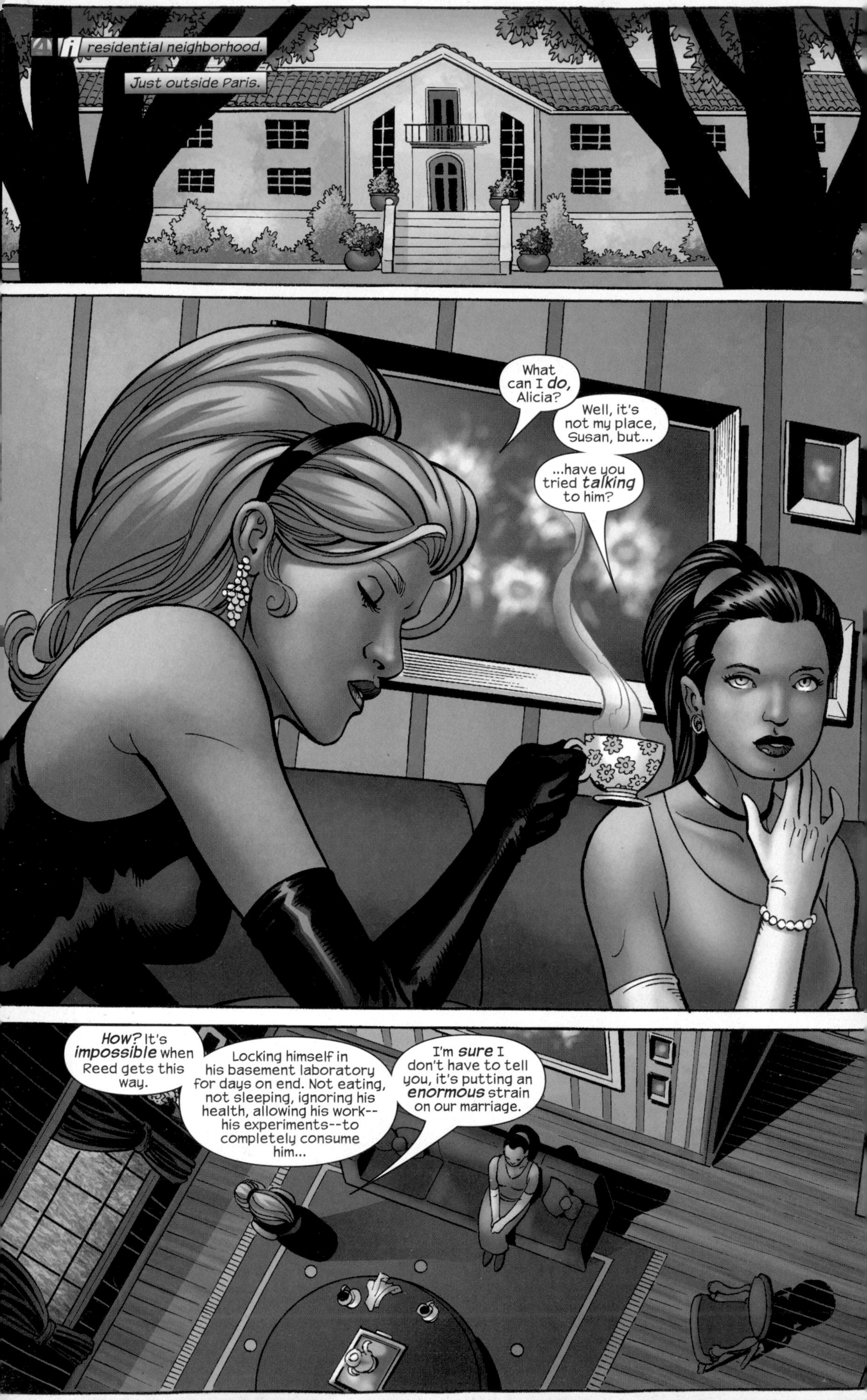
residential neighborhood.
Just outside Paris.
What can I *do*, Alicia?
Well, it's not my place, Susan, but...
...have you tried *talking* to him?
How? It's *impossible* when Reed gets this way.
Locking himself in his basement laboratory for days on end. Not eating, not sleeping, ignoring his health, allowing his work--his experiments--to completely consume him...
I'm *sure* I don't have to tell you, it's putting an *enormous* strain on our marriage.

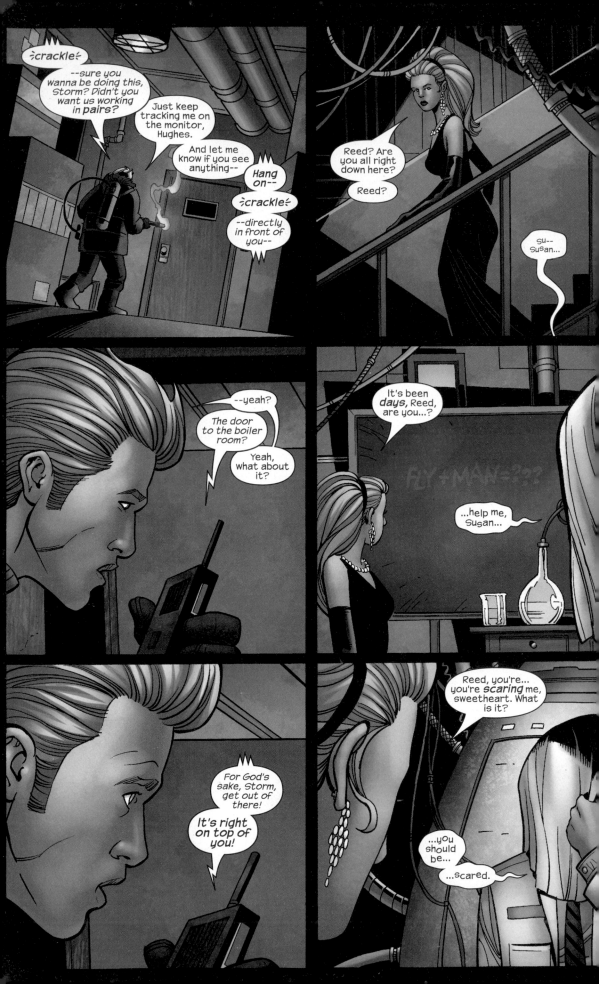

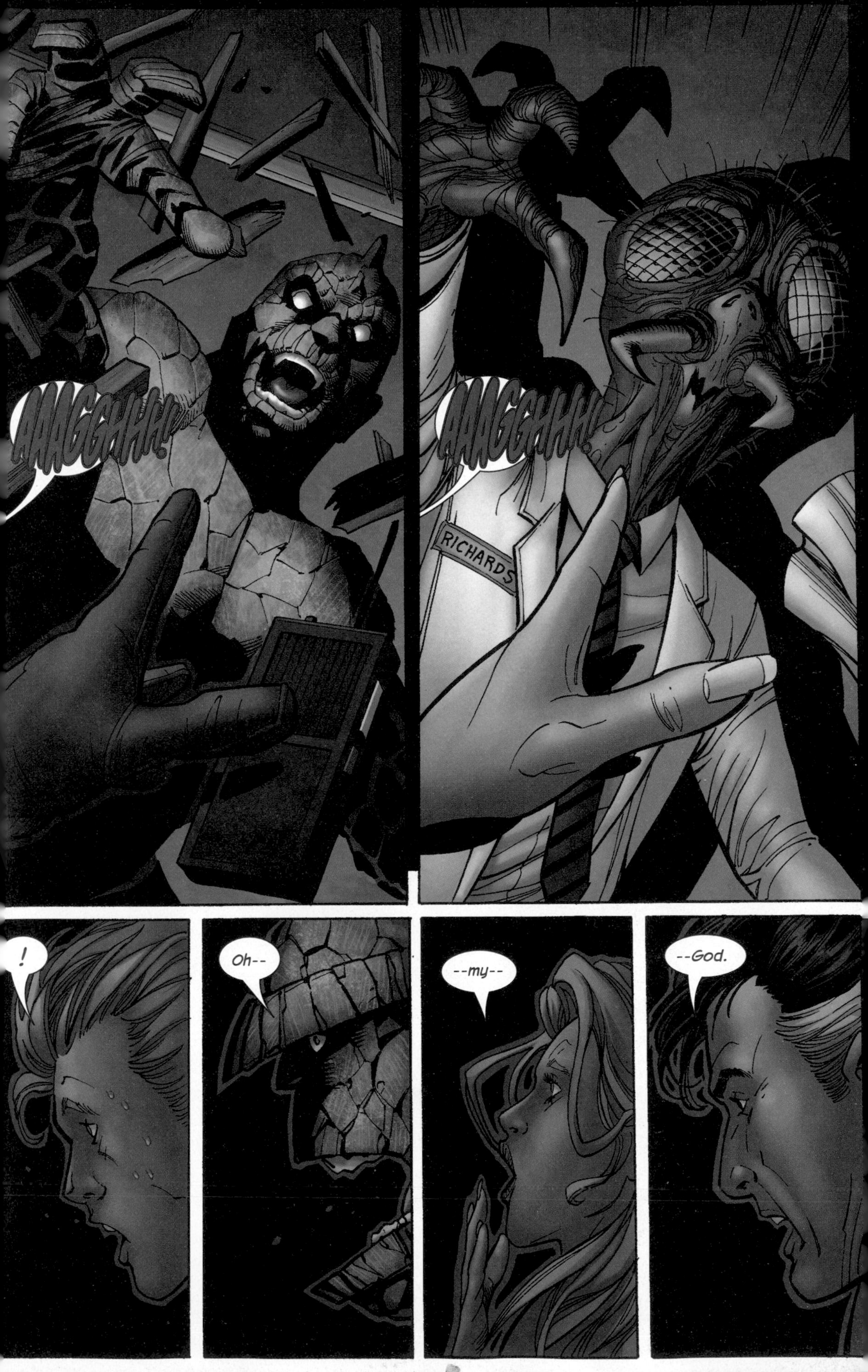
AAAGGHHH!
AAAGGHHH!
RICHARDS
!
Oh--
--my--
--God.

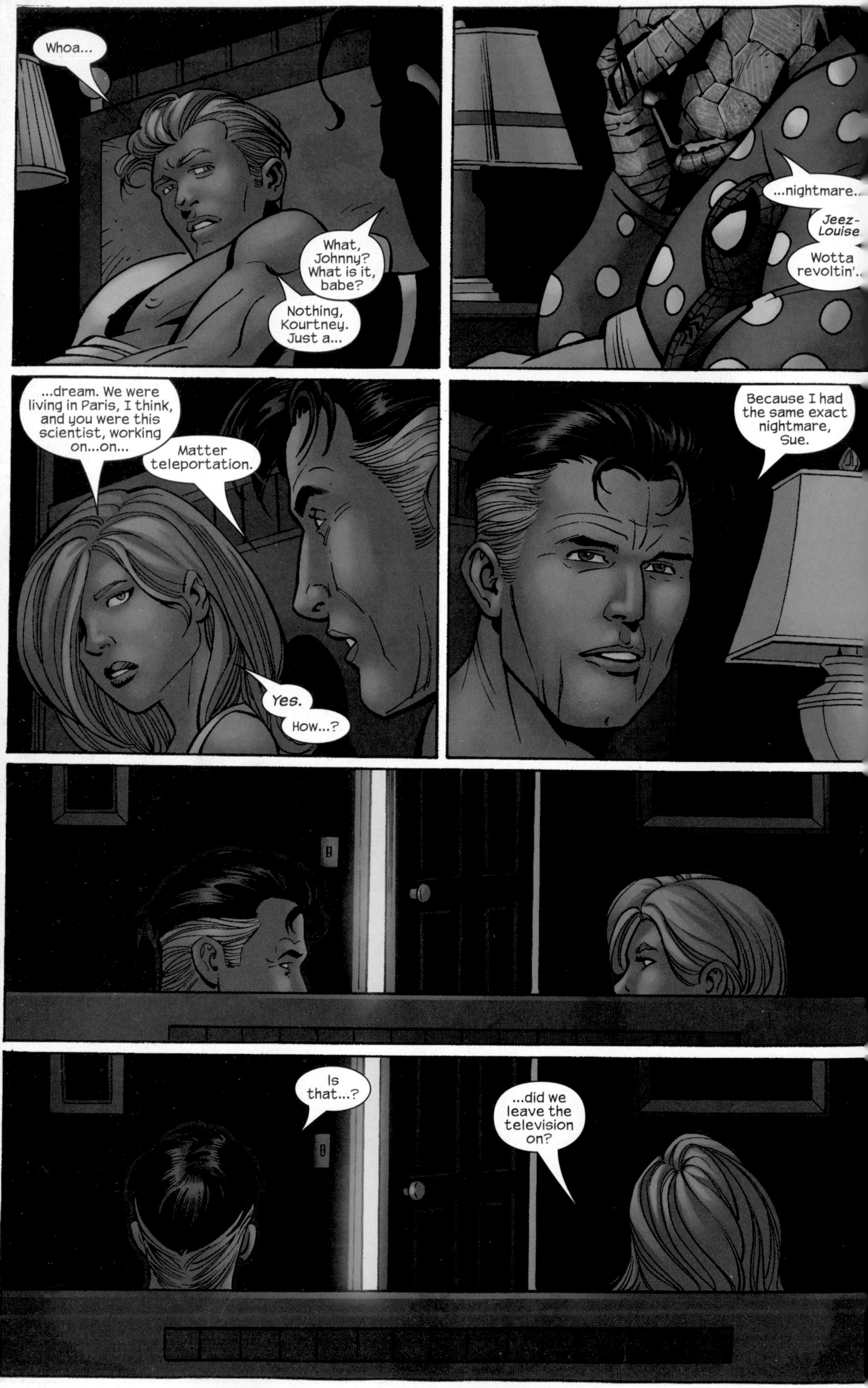
Whoa...
What, Johnny? What is it, babe?
Nothing, Kourtney. Just a...
...nightmare...
Jeez-Louise.
Wotta revoltin'...
...dream. We were living in Paris, I think, and you were this scientist, working on...on...
Matter teleportation.
Yes.
How...?
Because I had the same exact nightmare, Sue.
Is that...?
...did we leave the television on?

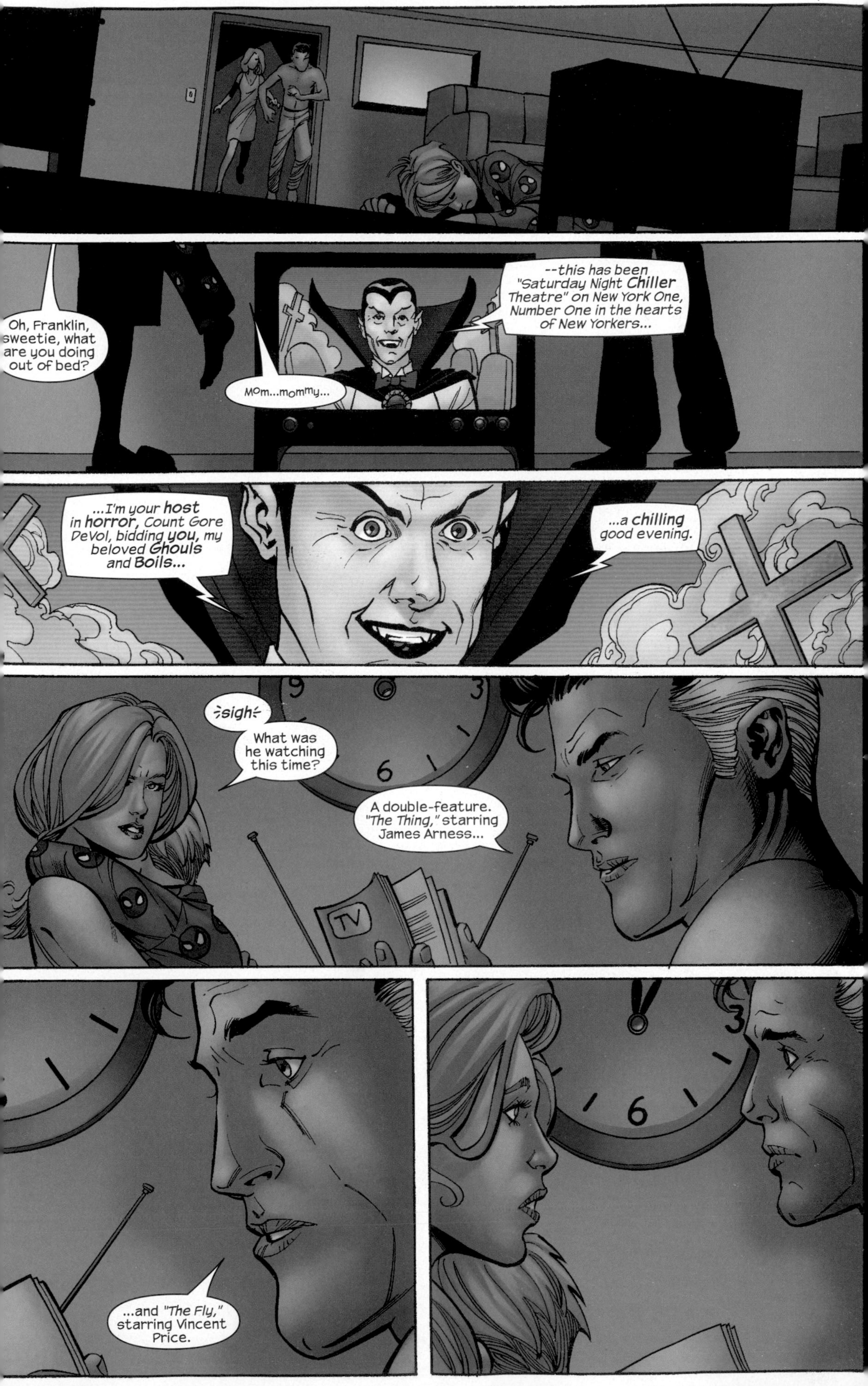

Oh, Franklin, sweetie, what are you doing out of bed?
Mom...mommy...
--this has been "Saturday Night Chiller Theatre" on New York One, Number One in the hearts of New Yorkers...
...I'm your host in horror, Count Gore DeVol, bidding you, my beloved Ghouls and Boils...
...a chilling good evening.
sigh
What was he watching this time?
A double-feature. "The Thing," starring James Arness...
TV
...and "The Fly," starring Vincent Price.

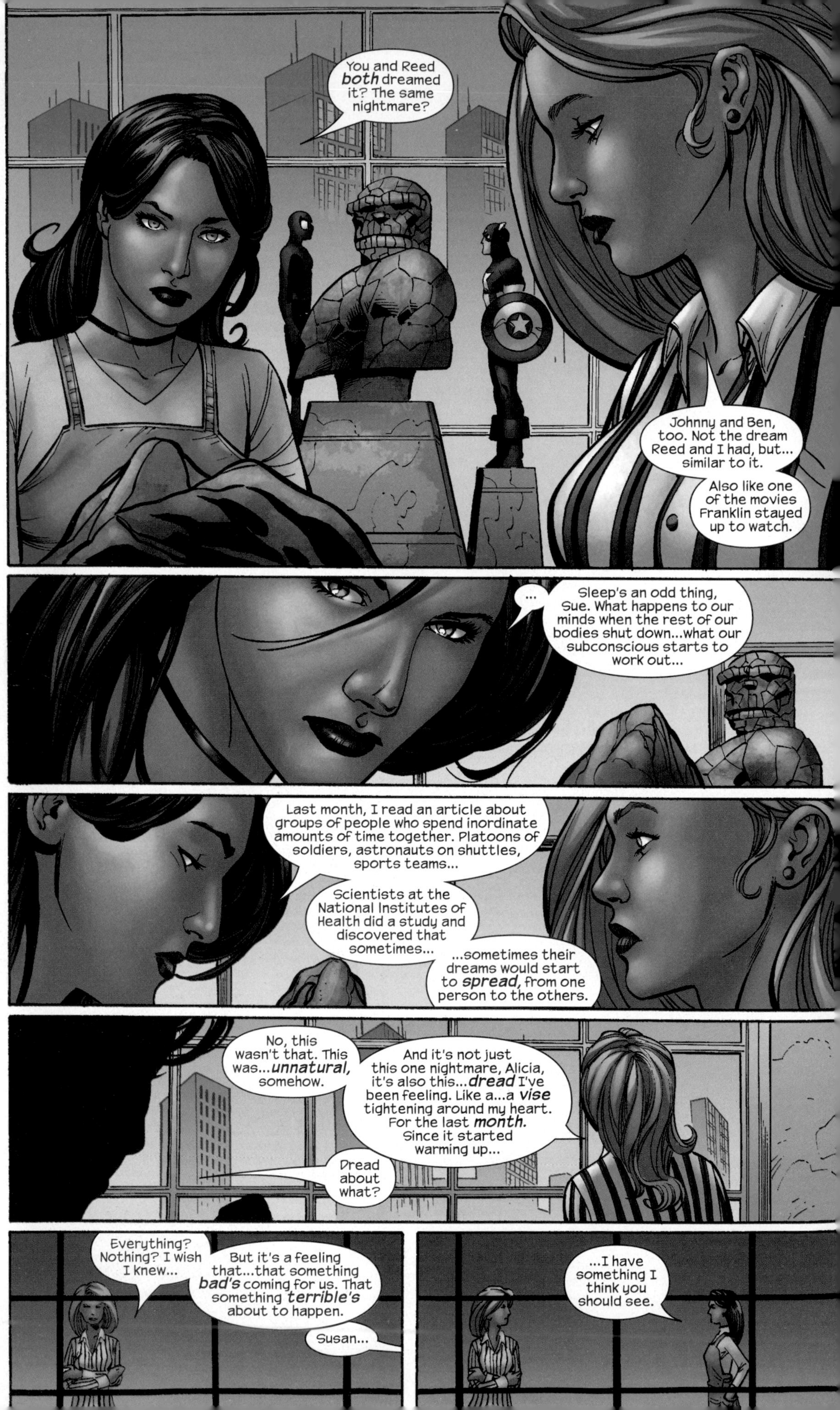

You and Reed both dreamed it? The same nightmare?
Johnny and Ben, too. Not the dream Reed and I had, but... similar to it.
Also like one of the movies Franklin stayed up to watch.
...
Sleep's an odd thing, Sue. What happens to our minds when the rest of our bodies shut down...what our subconscious starts to work out...
Last month, I read an article about groups of people who spend inordinate amounts of time together. Platoons of soldiers, astronauts on shuttles, sports teams...
Scientists at the National Institutes of Health did a study and discovered that sometimes...
...sometimes their dreams would start to spread, from one person to the others.
No, this wasn't that. This was...unnatural, somehow.
And it's not just this one nightmare, Alicia, it's also this...dread I've been feeling. Like a...a vise tightening around my heart. For the last month. Since it started warming up...
Dread about what?
Everything? Nothing? I wish I knew...
But it's a feeling that...that something bad's coming for us. That something terrible's about to happen.
Susan...
...I have something I think you should see.

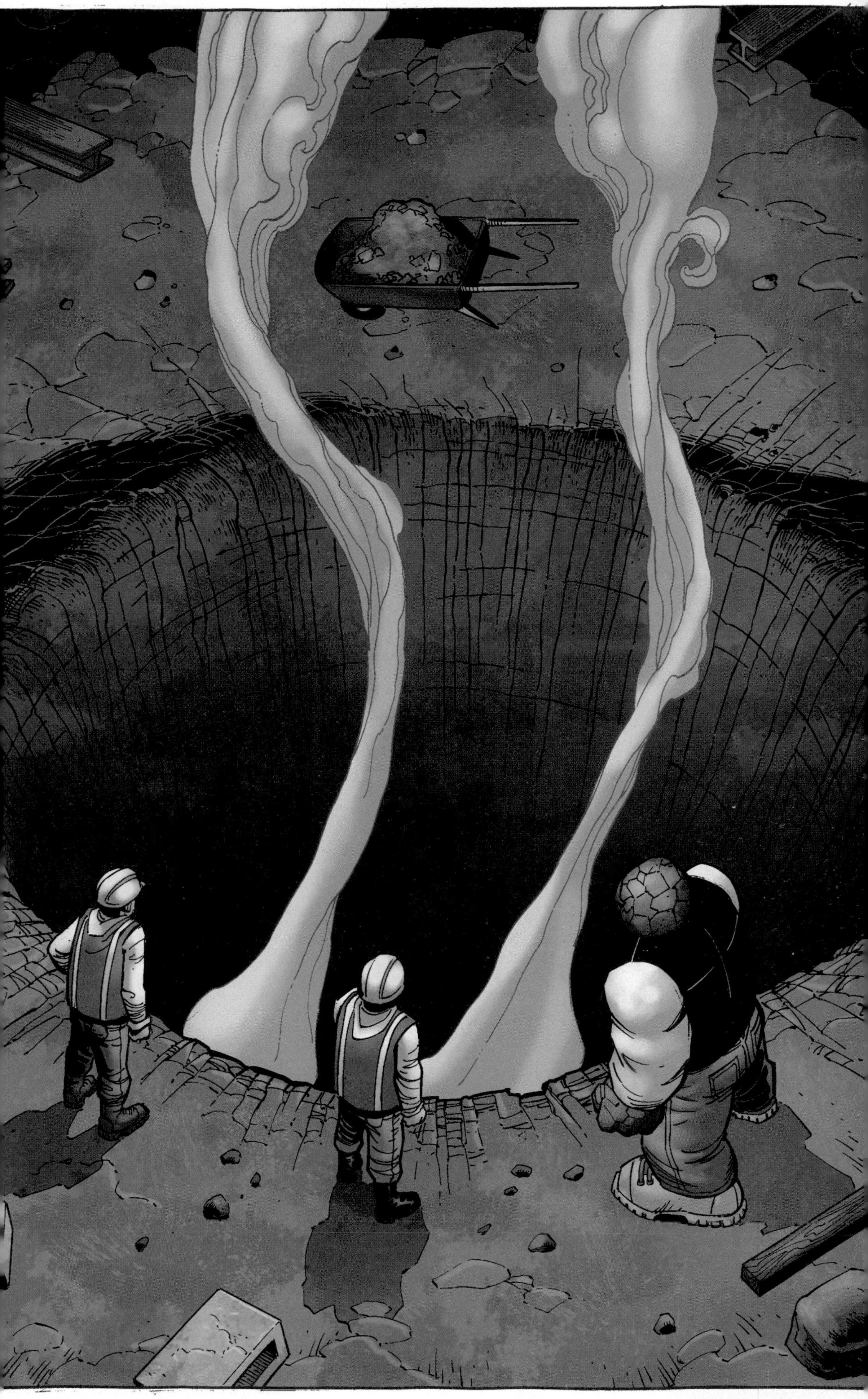

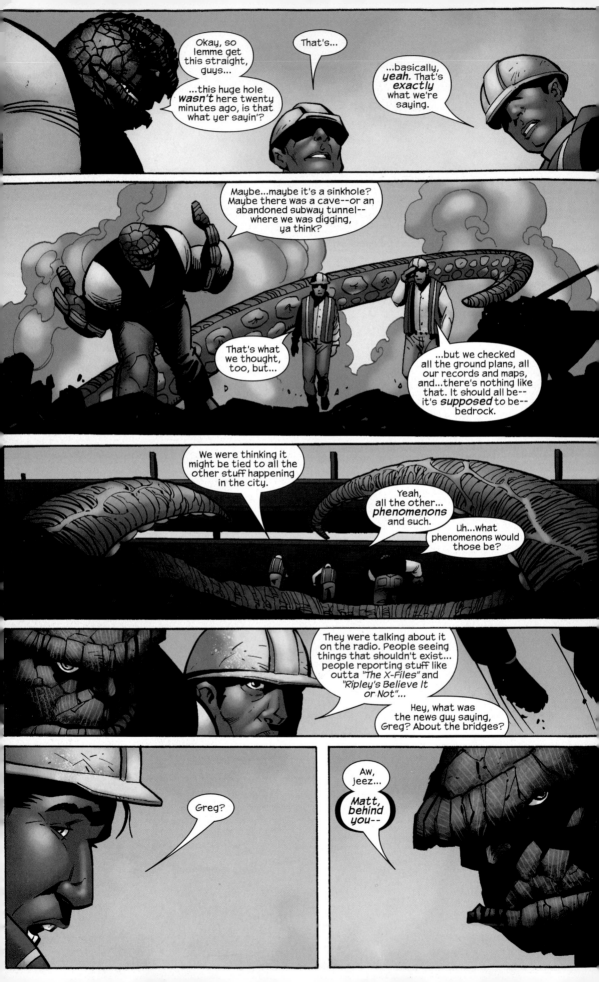

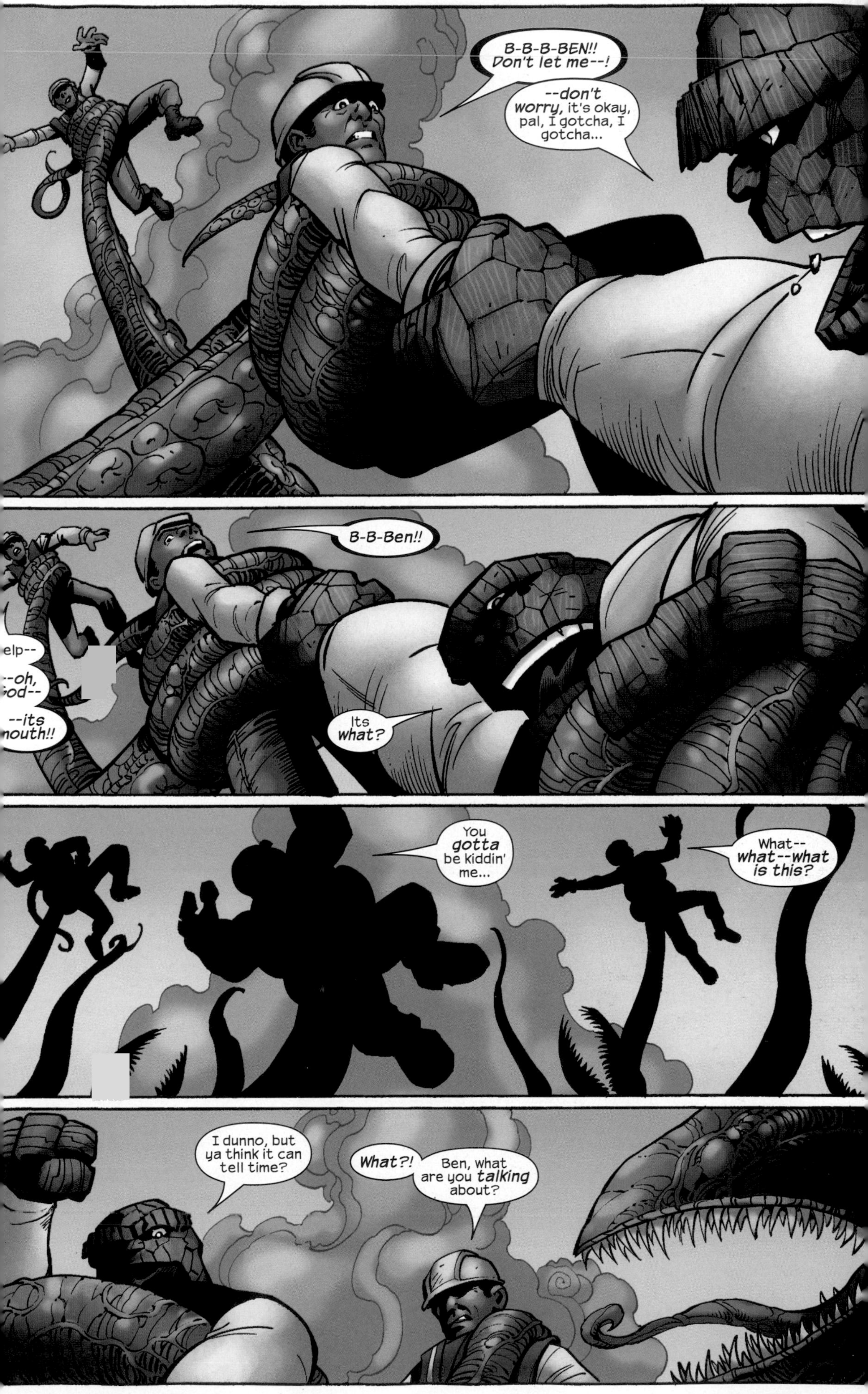
B-B-B-BEN!! Don't let me--!
--don't worry, it's okay, pal, I gotcha, I gotcha...
B-B-Ben!!
elp--
--oh, God--
--its mouth!!
Its what?
You gotta be kiddin' me...
What-- what--what is this?
I dunno, but ya think it can tell time?
What?!
Ben, what are you talking about?

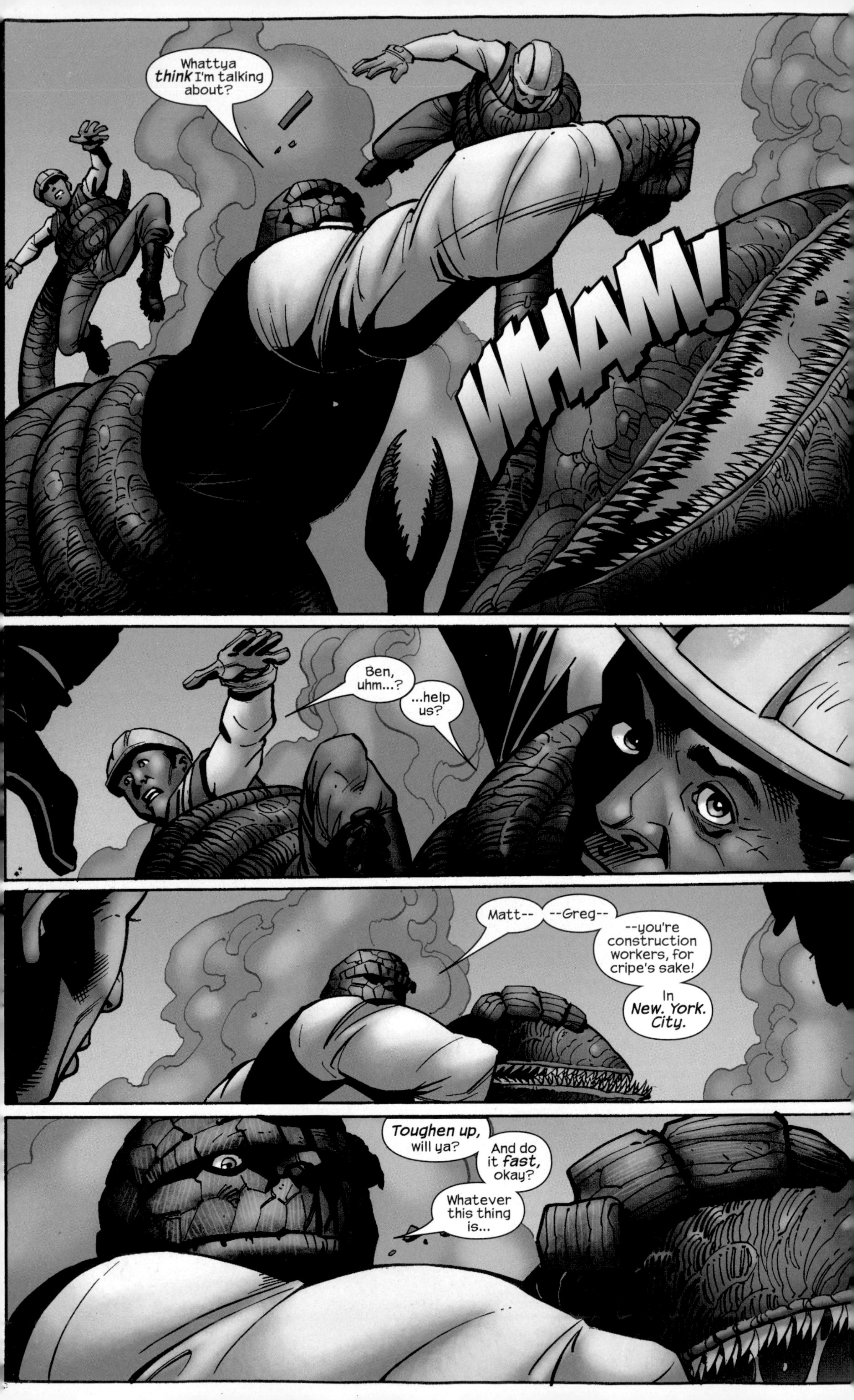
Whattya *think* I'm talking about?
WHAM!
Ben, uhm...?
...help us?
Matt--
--Greg--
--you're construction workers, for cripe's sake!
In *New. York. City.*
Toughen up, will ya?
And do it *fast,* okay?
Whatever this thing is...

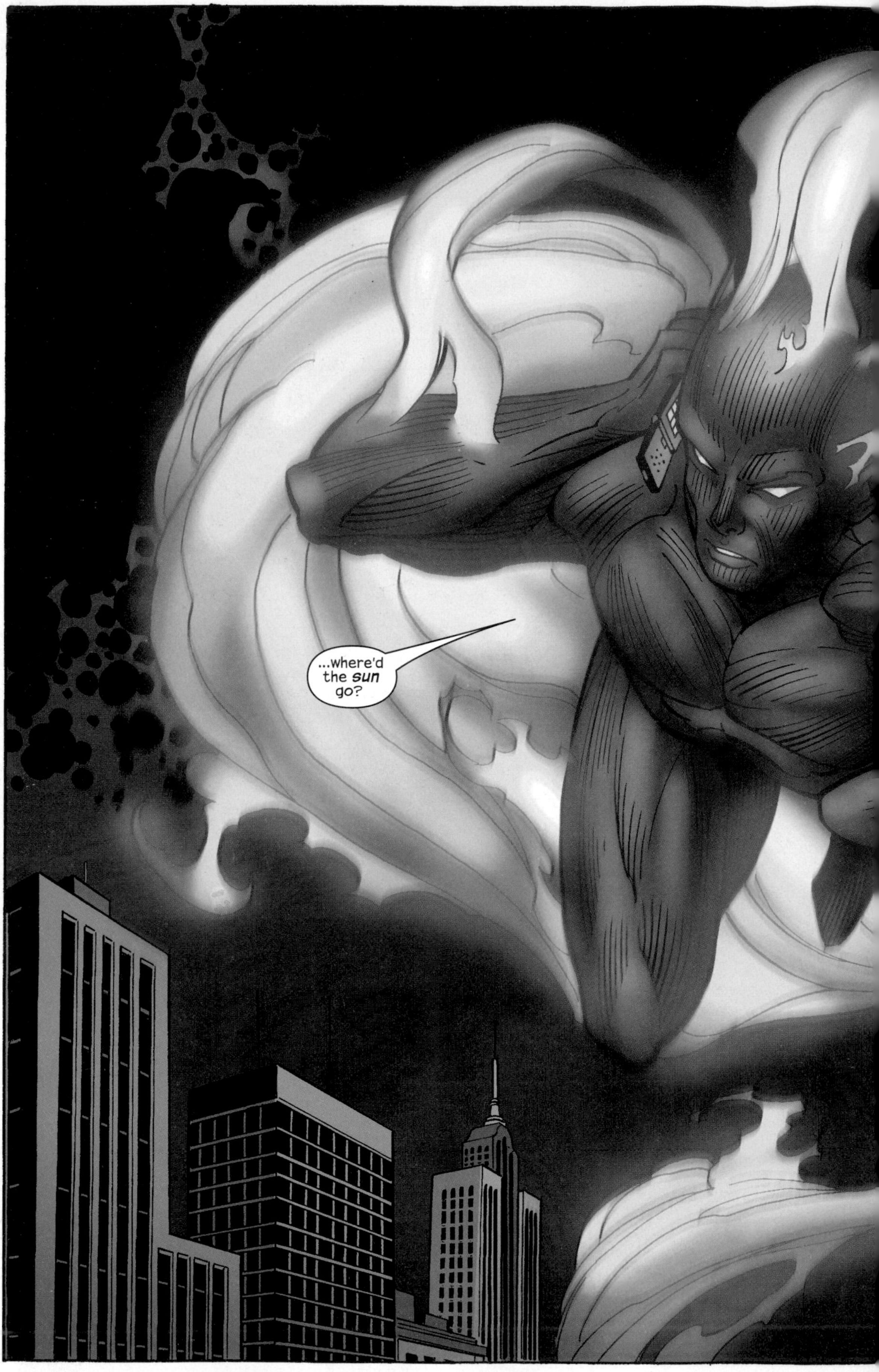
...where'd the *sun* go?

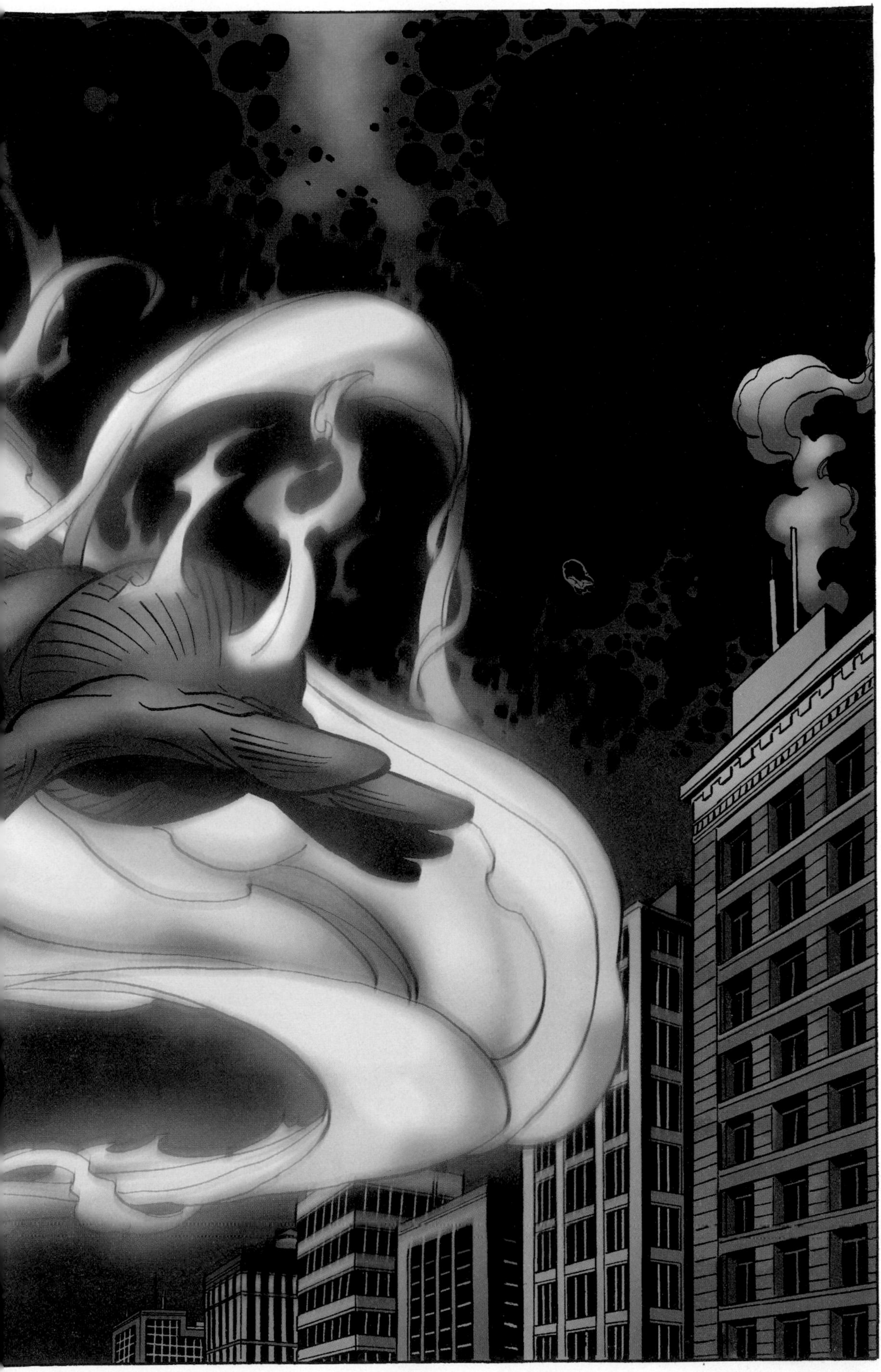

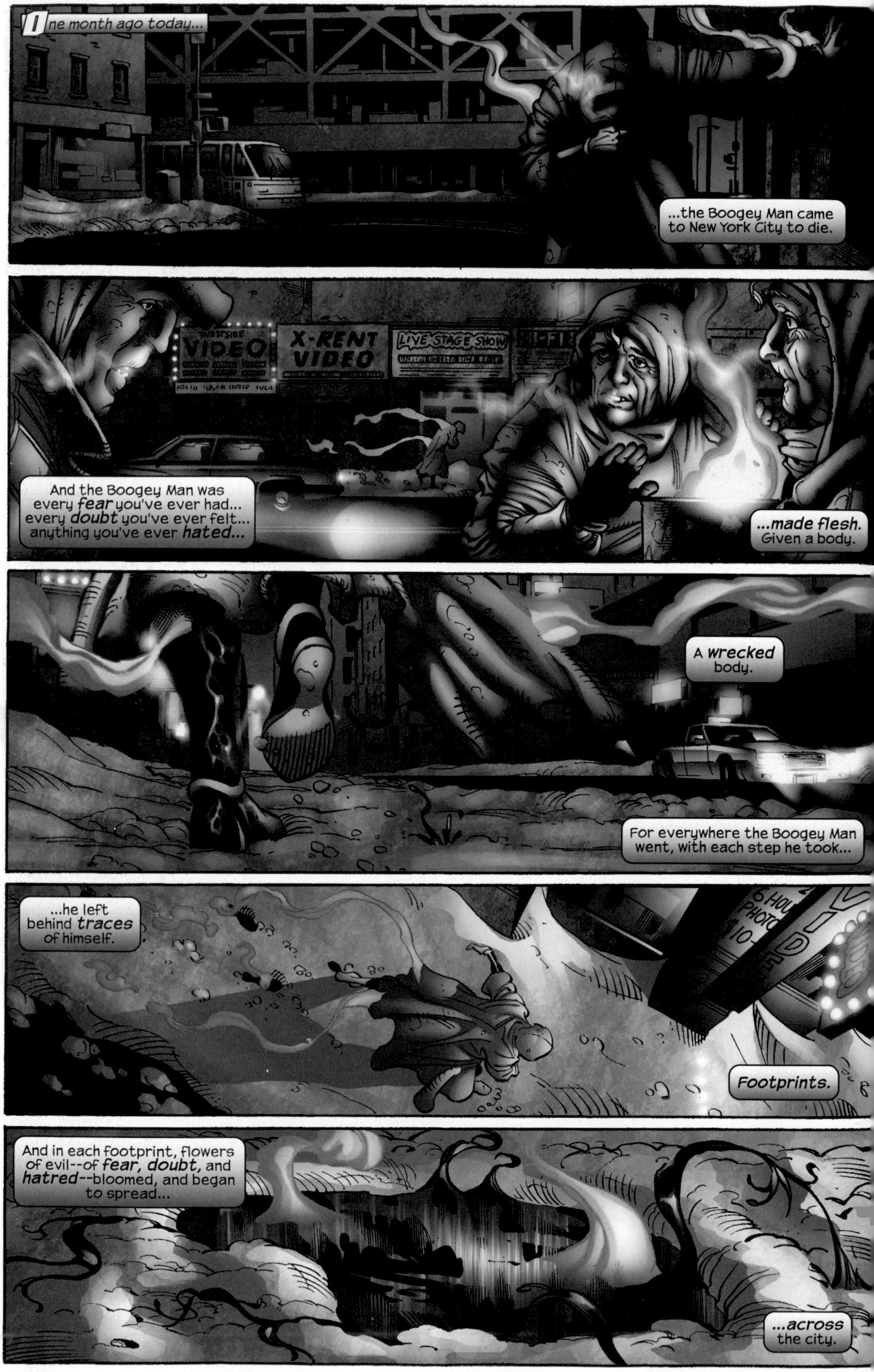
One month ago today...
...the Boogey Man came to New York City to die.
WESTSIDE VIDEO
X-RENT VIDEO
LIVE STAGE SHOW
And the Boogey Man was every fear you've ever had... every doubt you've ever felt... anything you've ever hated...
...made flesh. Given a body.
A wrecked body.
For everywhere the Boogey Man went, with each step he took...
...he left behind traces of himself.
Footprints.
And in each footprint, flowers of evil--of fear, doubt, and hatred--bloomed, and began to spread...
...across the city.

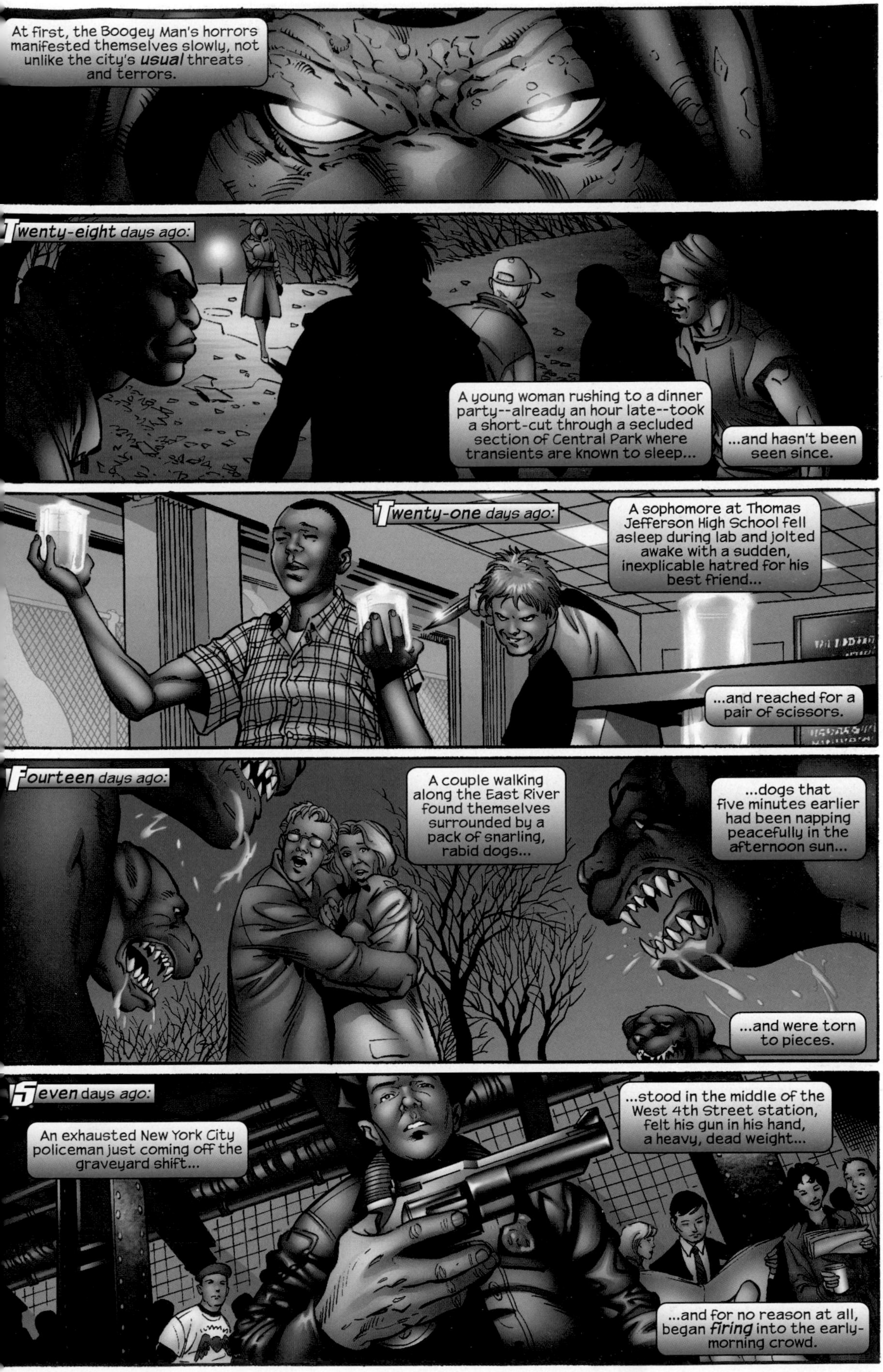
At first, the Boogey Man's horrors manifested themselves slowly, not unlike the city's *usual* threats and terrors.
Twenty-eight days ago:
A young woman rushing to a dinner party--already an hour late--took a short-cut through a secluded section of Central Park where transients are known to sleep...
...and hasn't been seen since.
Twenty-one days ago:
A sophomore at Thomas Jefferson High School fell asleep during lab and jolted awake with a sudden, inexplicable hatred for his best friend...
...and reached for a pair of scissors.
Fourteen days ago:
A couple walking along the East River found themselves surrounded by a pack of snarling, rabid dogs...
...dogs that five minutes earlier had been napping peacefully in the afternoon sun...
...and were torn to pieces.
Seven days ago:
An exhausted New York City policeman just coming off the graveyard shift...
...stood in the middle of the West 4th Street station, felt his gun in his hand, a heavy, dead weight...
...and for no reason at all, began *firing* into the early-morning crowd.

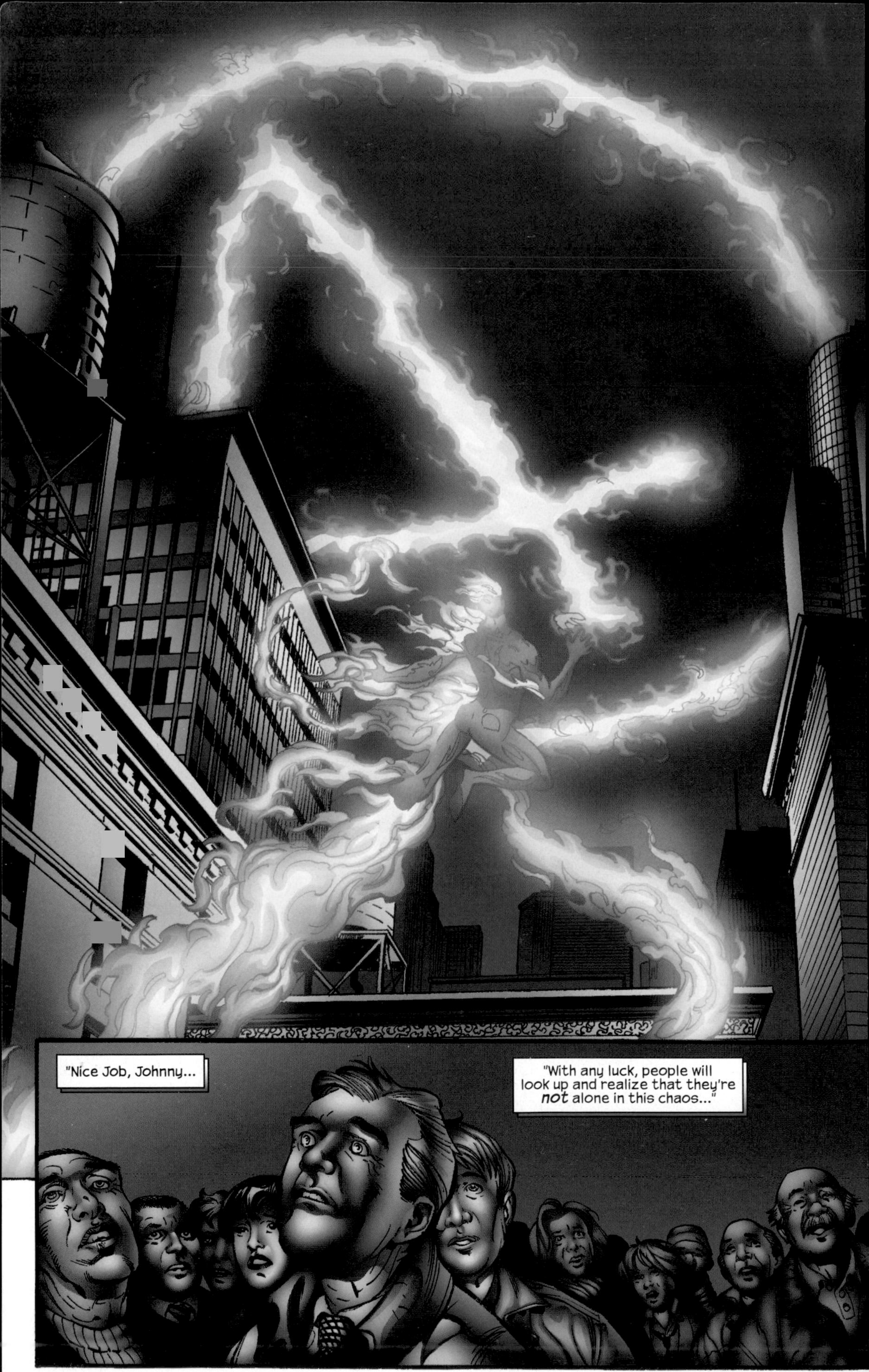
"Nice Job, Johnny...
"With any luck, people will look up and realize that they're *not* alone in this chaos..."

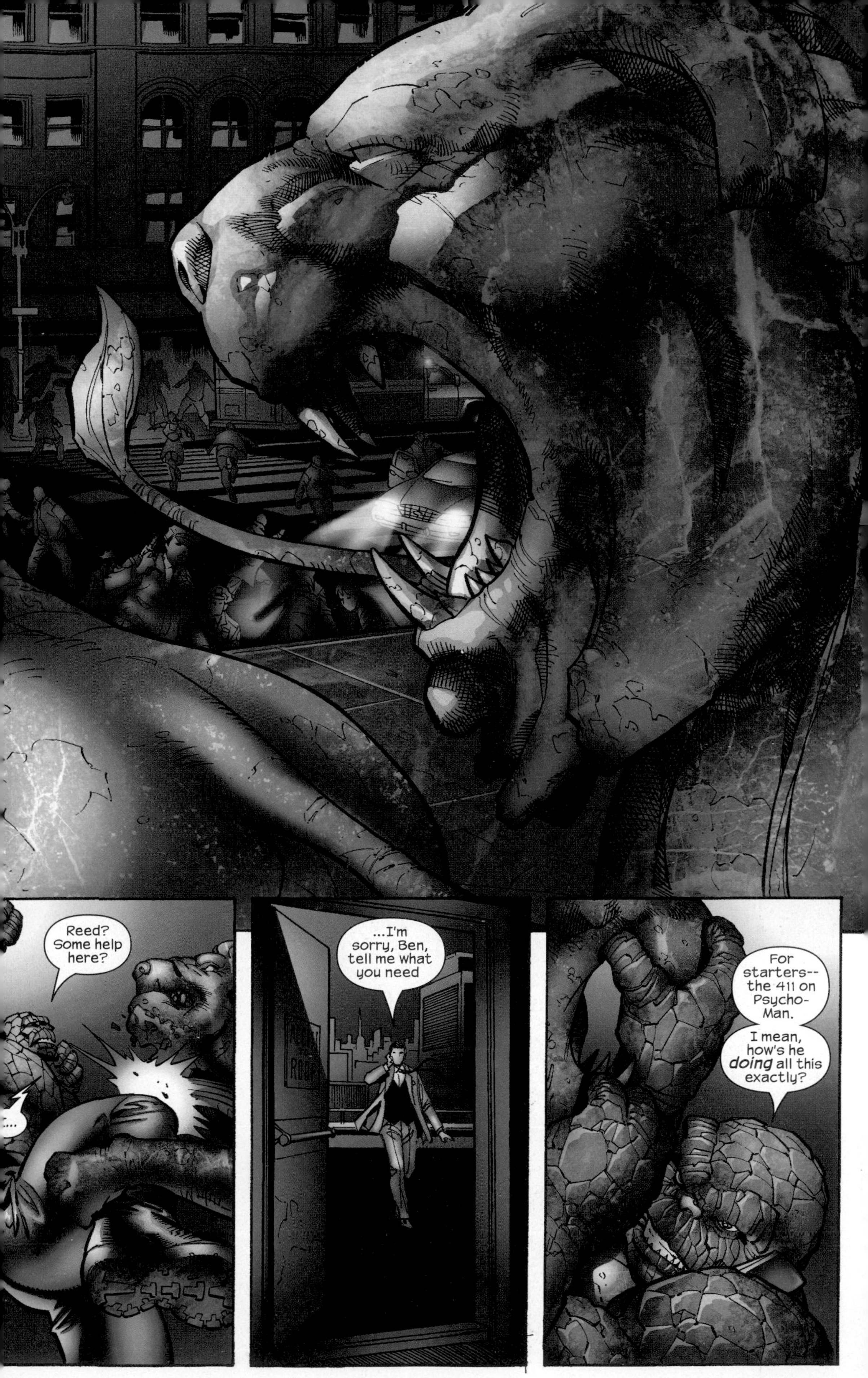
Reed? Some help here?
...I'm sorry, Ben, tell me what you need
For starters-- the 411 on Psycho-Man.
I mean, how's he *doing* all this exactly?

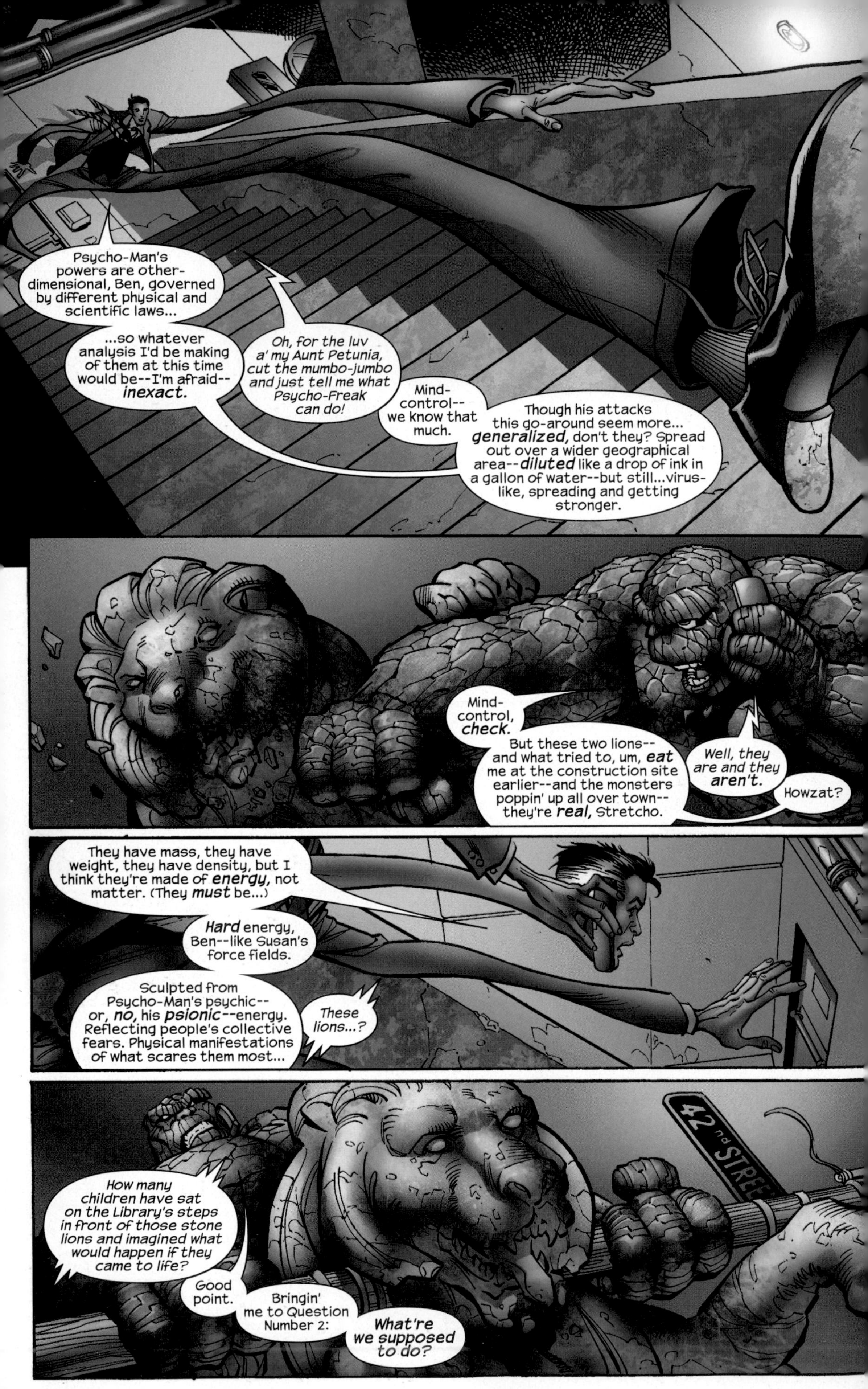

Psycho-Man's powers are other-dimensional, Ben, governed by different physical and scientific laws...
...so whatever analysis I'd be making of them at this time would be--I'm afraid--*inexact.*
Oh, for the luv a' my Aunt Petunia, cut the mumbo-jumbo and just tell me what Psycho-Freak can do!
Mind-control--we know that much.
Though his attacks this go-around seem more... ***generalized,*** don't they? Spread out over a wider geographical area--***diluted*** like a drop of ink in a gallon of water--but still...virus-like, spreading and getting stronger.
Mind-control, ***check.***
But these two lions--and what tried to, um, ***eat*** me at the construction site earlier--and the monsters poppin' up all over town--they're ***real,*** Stretcho.
*Well, they are and they **aren't.***
Howzat?
They have mass, they have weight, they have density, but I think they're made of ***energy,*** not matter. (They ***must*** be...)
Hard energy, Ben--like Susan's force fields.
Sculpted from Psycho-Man's psychic--or, ***no,*** his ***psionic***--energy. Reflecting people's collective fears. Physical manifestations of what scares them most...
These lions...?
42nd STREE
How many children have sat on the Library's steps in front of those stone lions and imagined what would happen if they came to life?
Good point.
Bringin' me to Question Number 2:
What're we supposed to do?

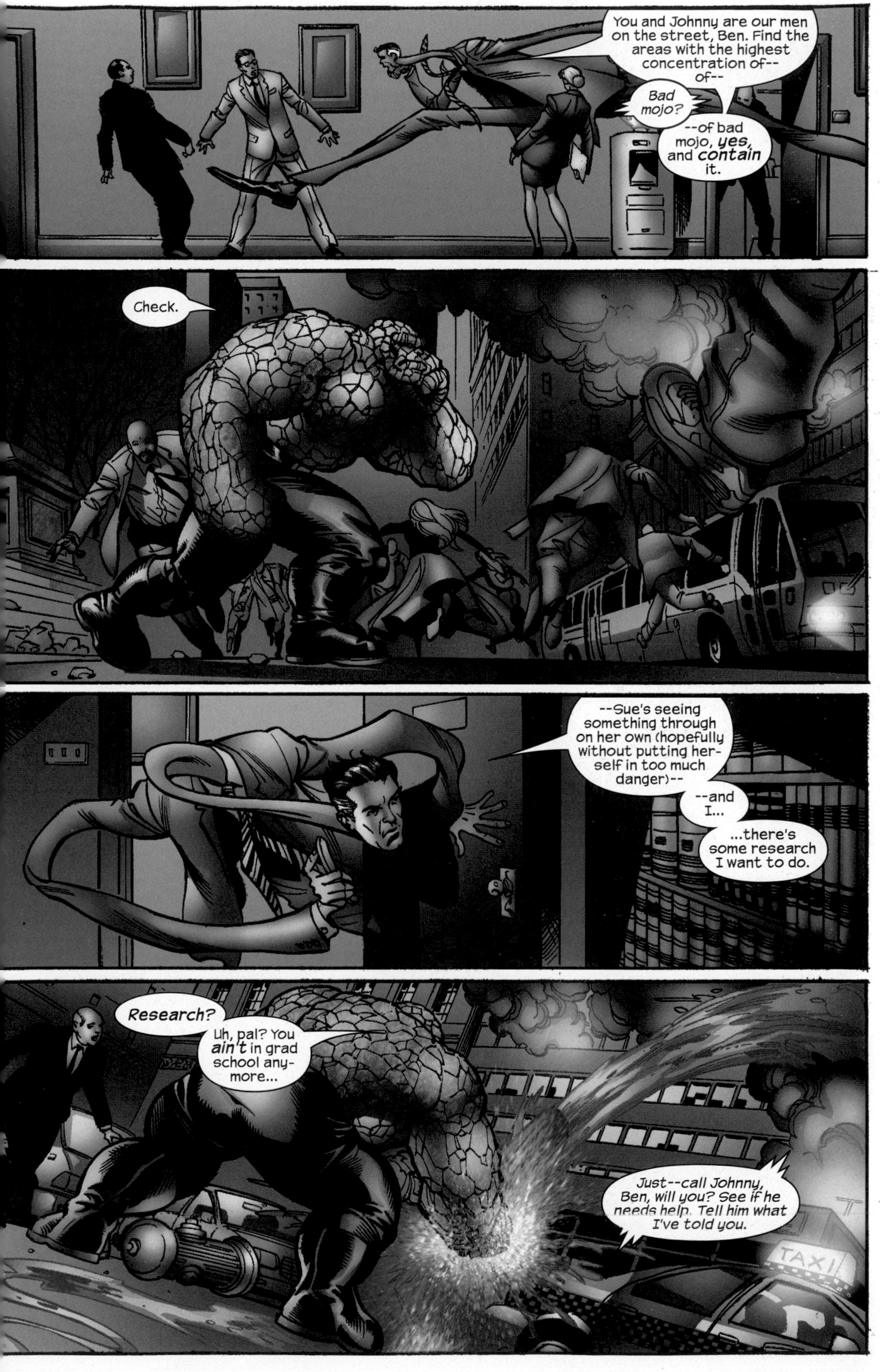
You and Johnny are our men on the street, Ben. Find the areas with the highest concentration of-- of--
Bad mojo?
--of bad mojo, *yes*, and *contain* it.
Check.
--Sue's seeing something through on her own (hopefully without putting her-self in too much danger)--
--and I...
...there's some research I want to do.
Research?
Uh, pal? You *ain't* in grad school any-more...
Just--call Johnny, Ben, will you? See if he needs help. Tell him what I've told you.
TAXI

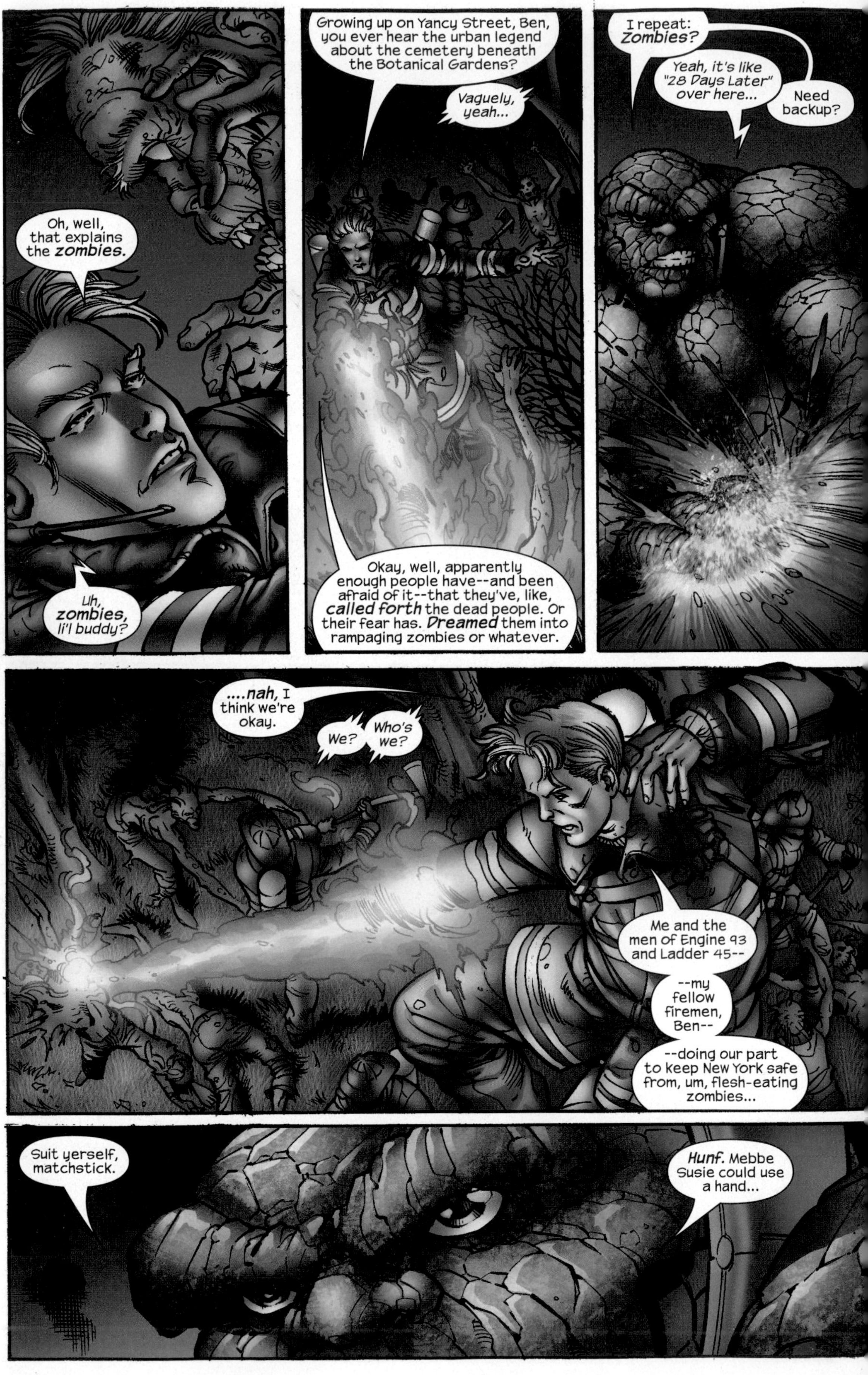

Oh, well, that explains the *zombies.*
Uh, **zombies,** li'l buddy?
Growing up on Yancy Street, Ben, you ever hear the urban legend about the cemetery beneath the Botanical Gardens?
Vaguely, yeah...
Okay, well, apparently enough people have--and been afraid of it--that they've, like, ***called forth*** the dead people. Or their fear has. ***Dreamed*** them into rampaging zombies or whatever.
I repeat: ***Zombies?***
Yeah, it's like "28 Days Later" over here...
Need backup?
....***nah,*** I think we're okay.
We?
Who's we?
Me and the men of Engine 93 and Ladder 45--
--my fellow firemen, Ben--
--doing our part to keep New York safe from, um, flesh-eating zombies...
Suit yerself, matchstick.
Hunf. Mebbe Susie could use a hand...

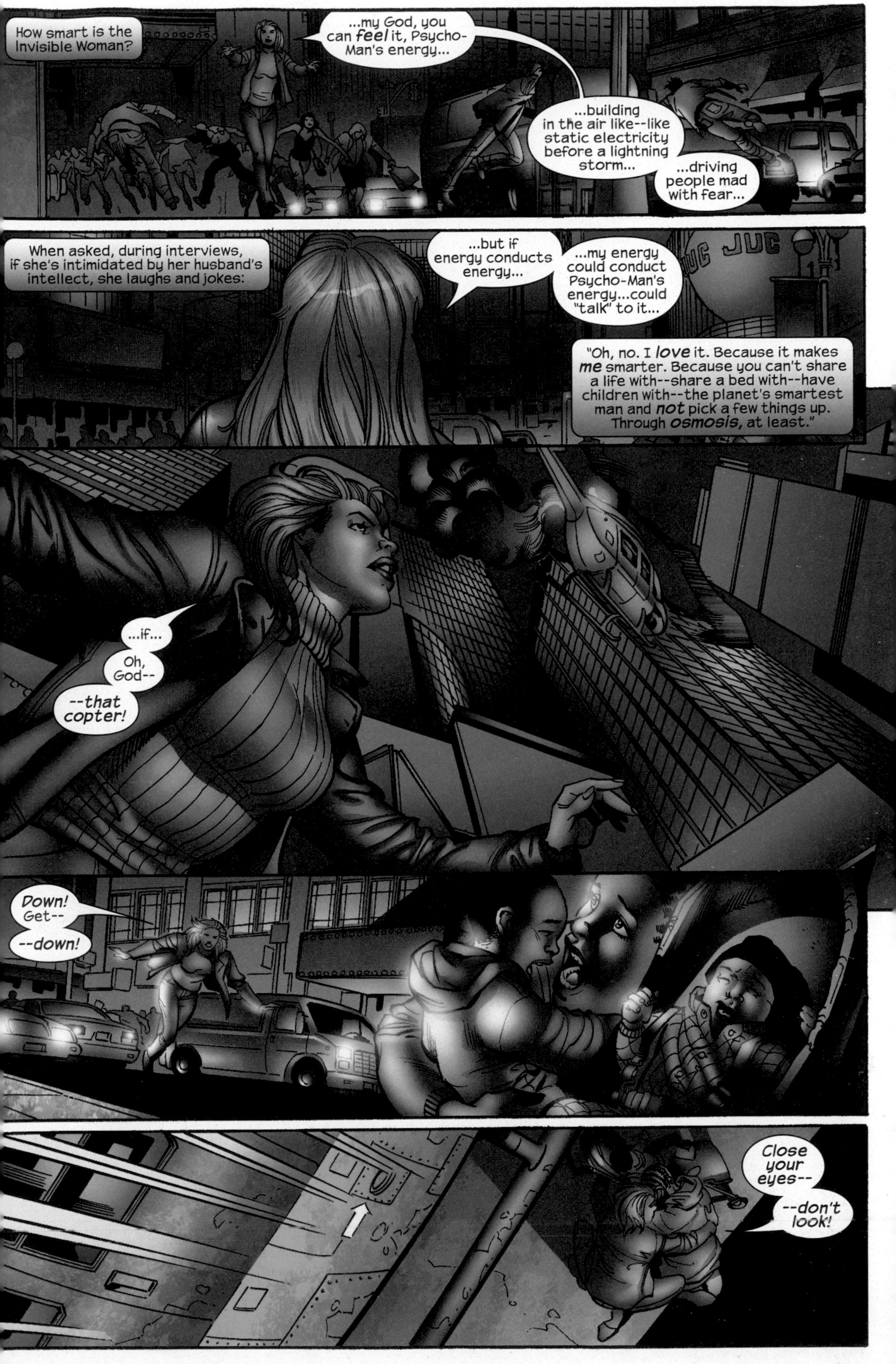

How smart is the Invisible Woman?
...my God, you can feel it, Psycho-Man's energy...
...building in the air like--like static electricity before a lightning storm...
...driving people mad with fear...
When asked, during interviews, if she's intimidated by her husband's intellect, she laughs and jokes:
...but if energy conducts energy...
...my energy could conduct Psycho-Man's energy...could "talk" to it...
"Oh, no. I love it. Because it makes me smarter. Because you can't share a life with--share a bed with--have children with--the planet's smartest man and not pick a few things up. Through osmosis, at least."
...if...
Oh, God--
--that copter!
Down! Get--
--down!
Close your eyes--
--don't look!

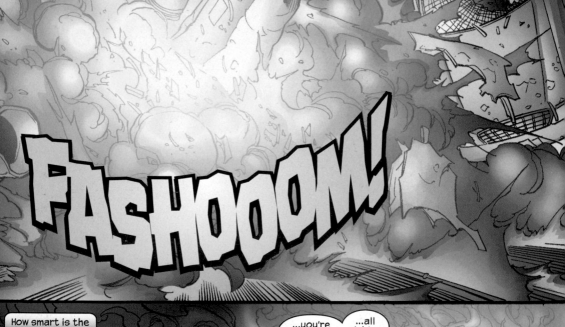

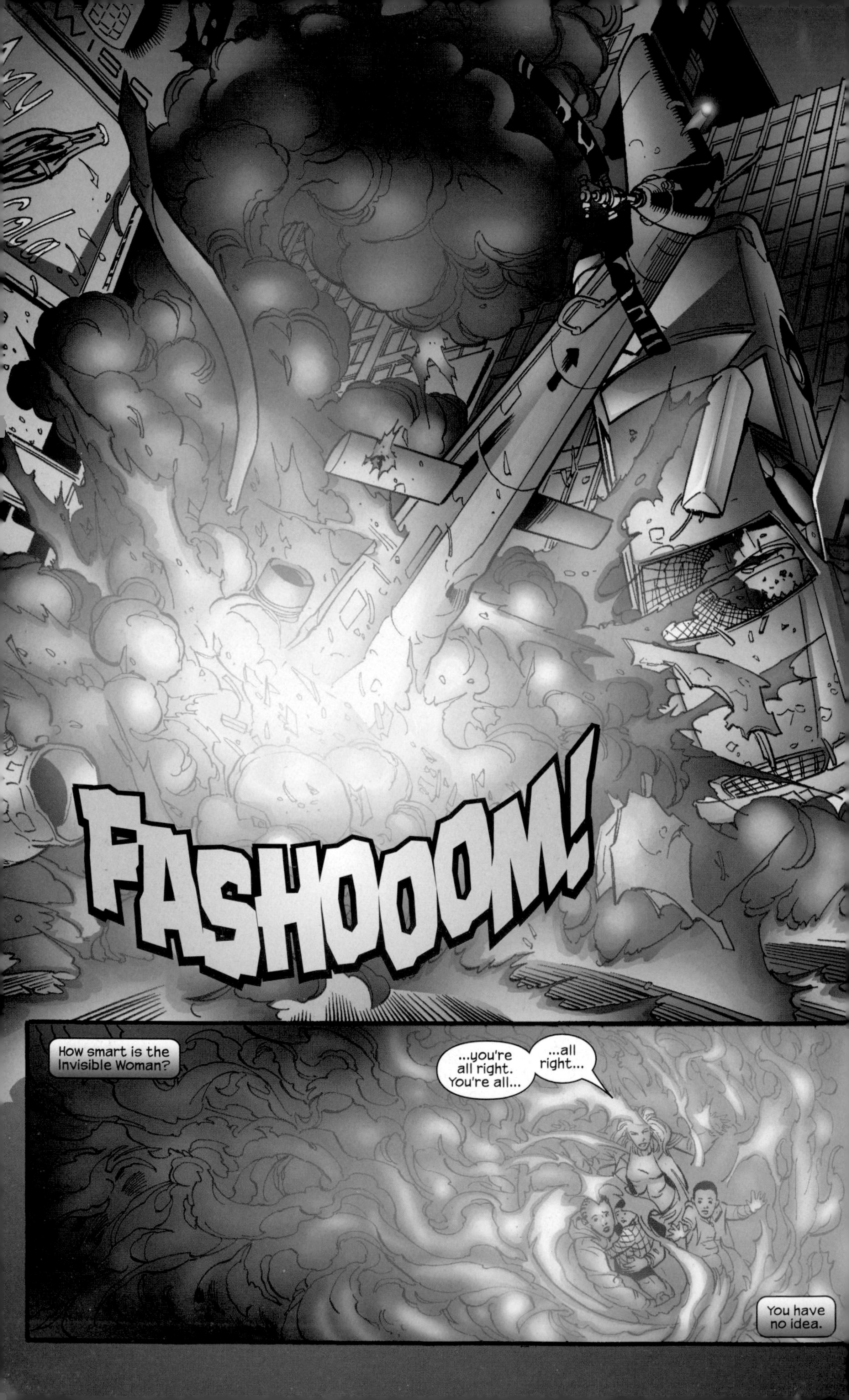
FASHOOOM!
How smart is the Invisible Woman?
...you're all right. You're all...
...all right...
You have no idea.

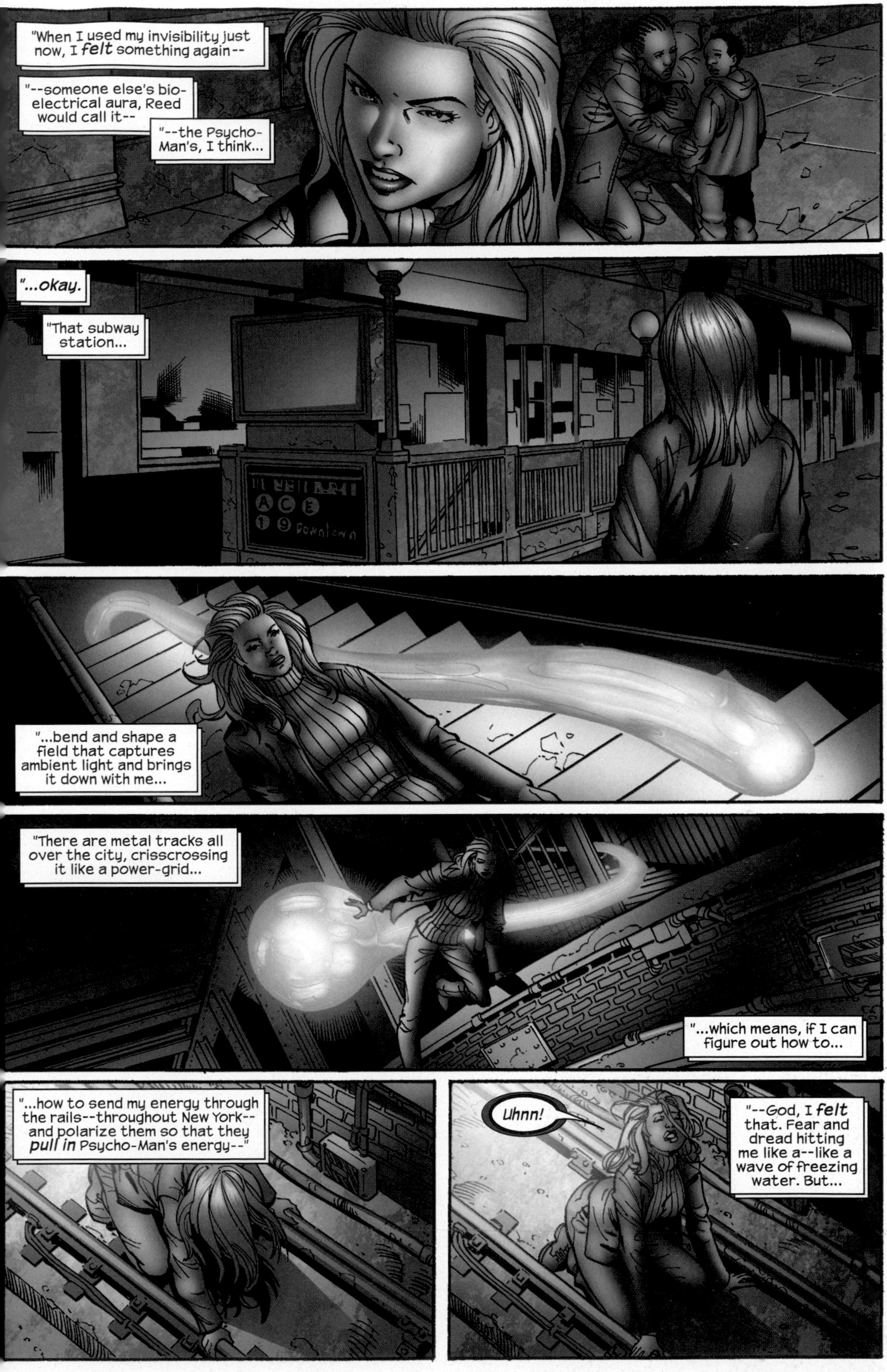
"When I used my invisibility just now, I felt something again--
"--someone else's bio-electrical aura, Reed would call it--
"--the Psycho-Man's, I think...
"...okay.
"That subway station...
A C E
1 9 DOWNTOWN
"...bend and shape a field that captures ambient light and brings it down with me...
"There are metal tracks all over the city, crisscrossing it like a power-grid...
"...which means, if I can figure out how to...
"...how to send my energy through the rails--throughout New York--and polarize them so that they pull in Psycho-Man's energy--"
Uhnn!
"--God, I felt that. Fear and dread hitting me like a--like a wave of freezing water. But...

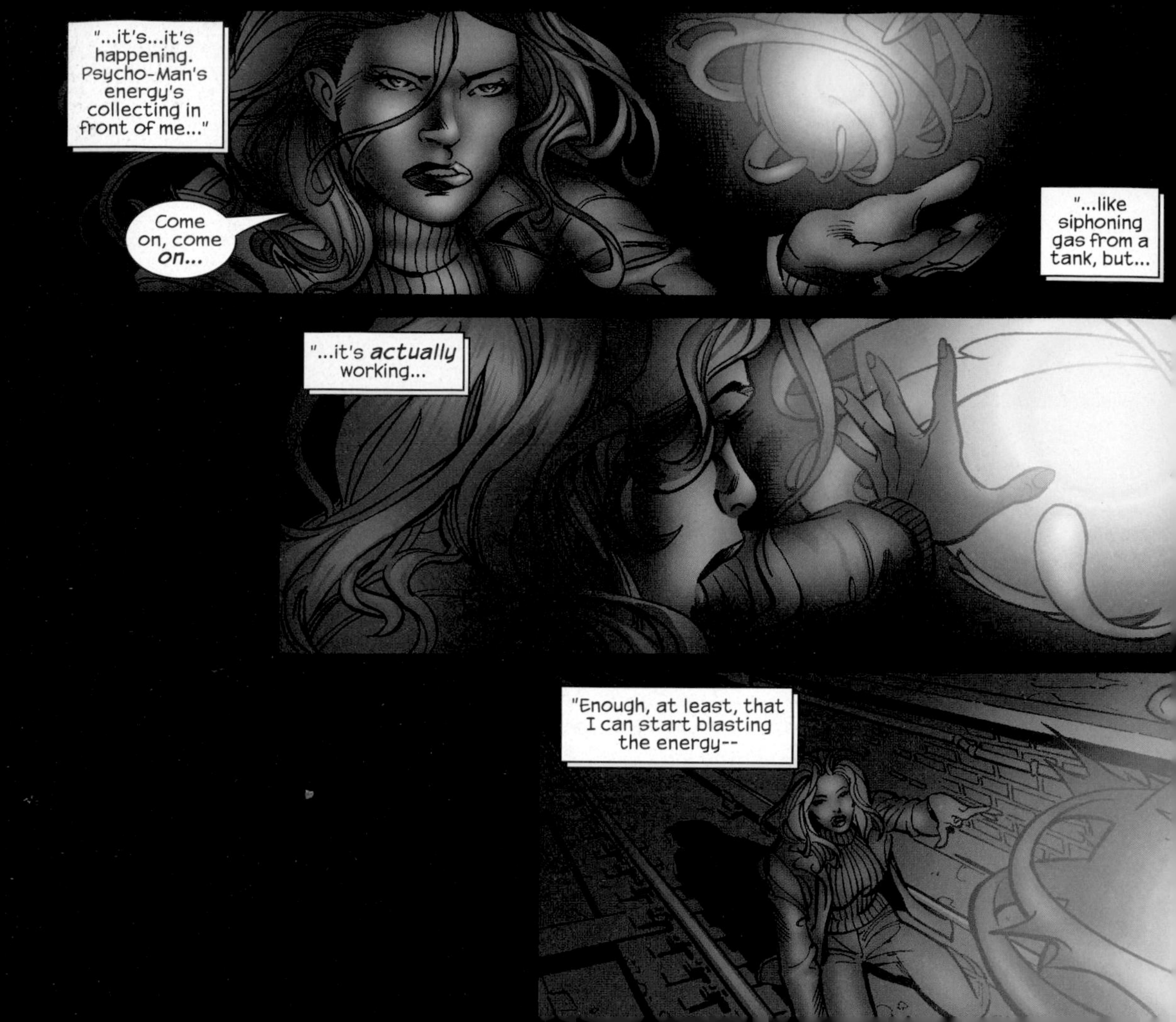
"...it's...it's happening. Psycho-Man's energy's collecting in front of me..."
Come on, come on...
"...like siphoning gas from a tank, but...
"...it's actually working...
"Enough, at least, that I can start blasting the energy--

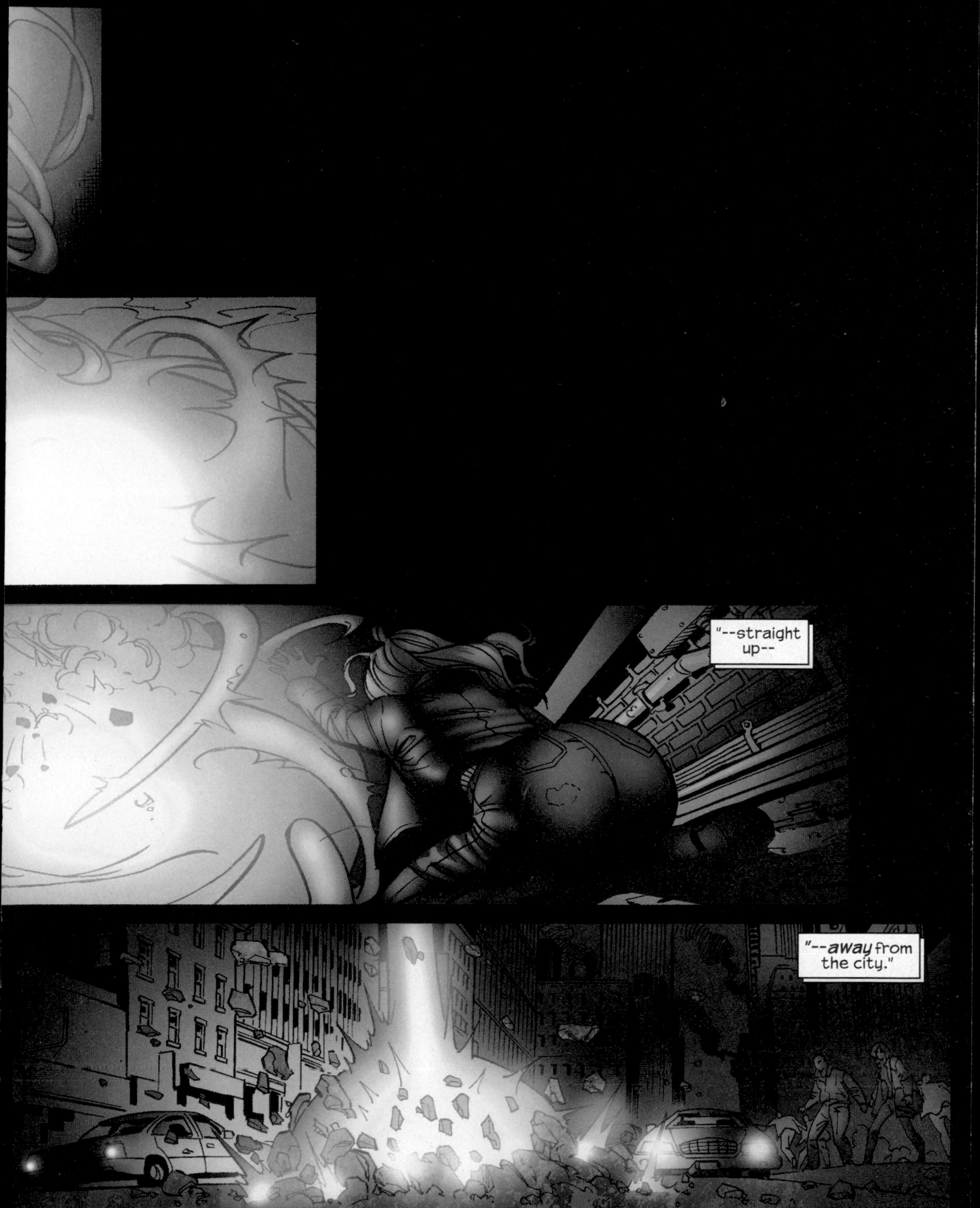
"--straight up--
"--*away* from the city."

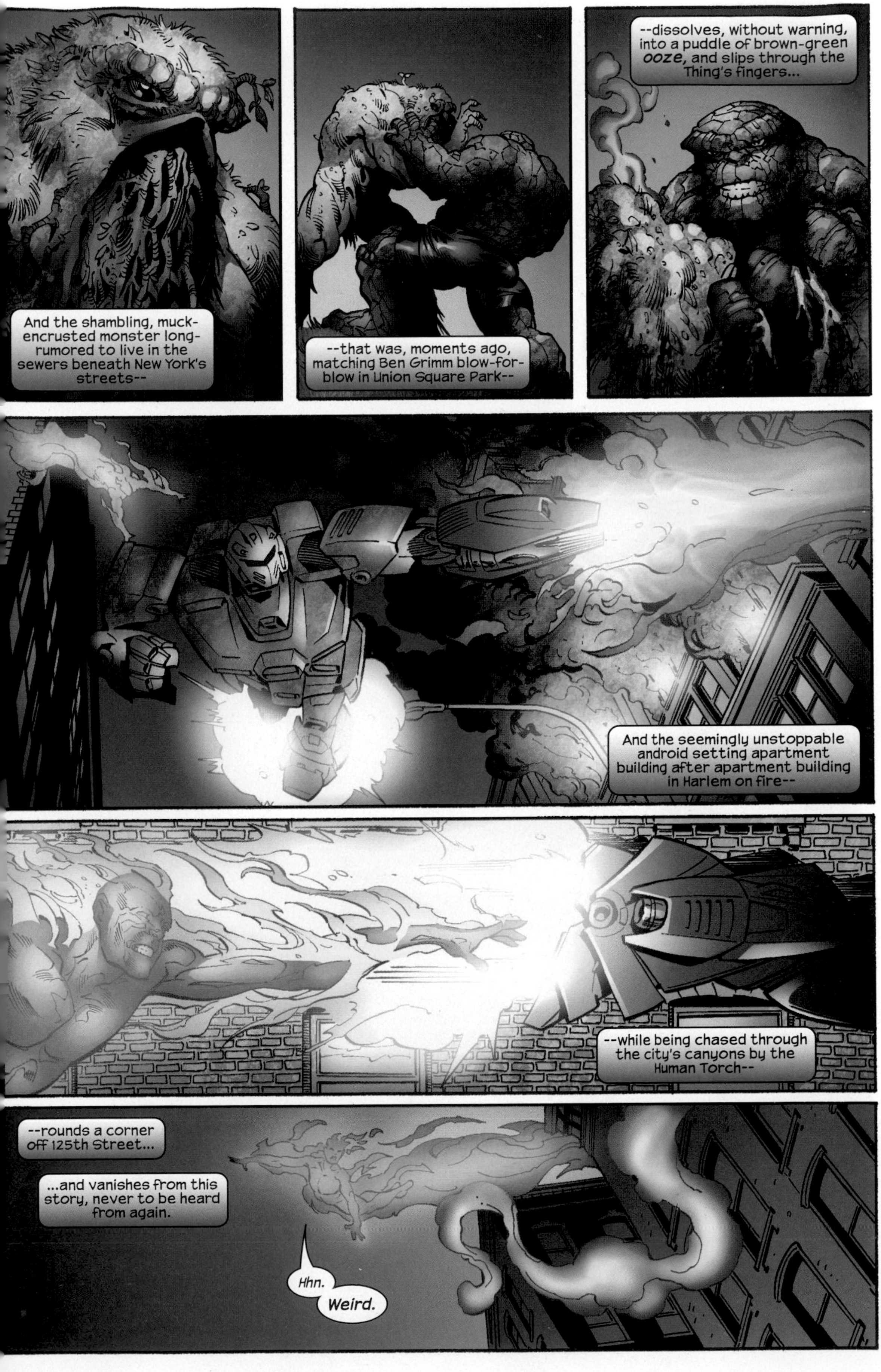
And the shambling, muck-encrusted monster long-rumored to live in the sewers beneath New York's streets--
--that was, moments ago, matching Ben Grimm blow-for-blow in Union Square Park--
--dissolves, without warning, into a puddle of brown-green ooze, and slips through the Thing's fingers...
And the seemingly unstoppable android setting apartment building after apartment building in Harlem on fire--
--while being chased through the city's canyons by the Human Torch--
--rounds a corner off 125th Street...
...and vanishes from this story, never to be heard from again.
Hhn.
Weird.

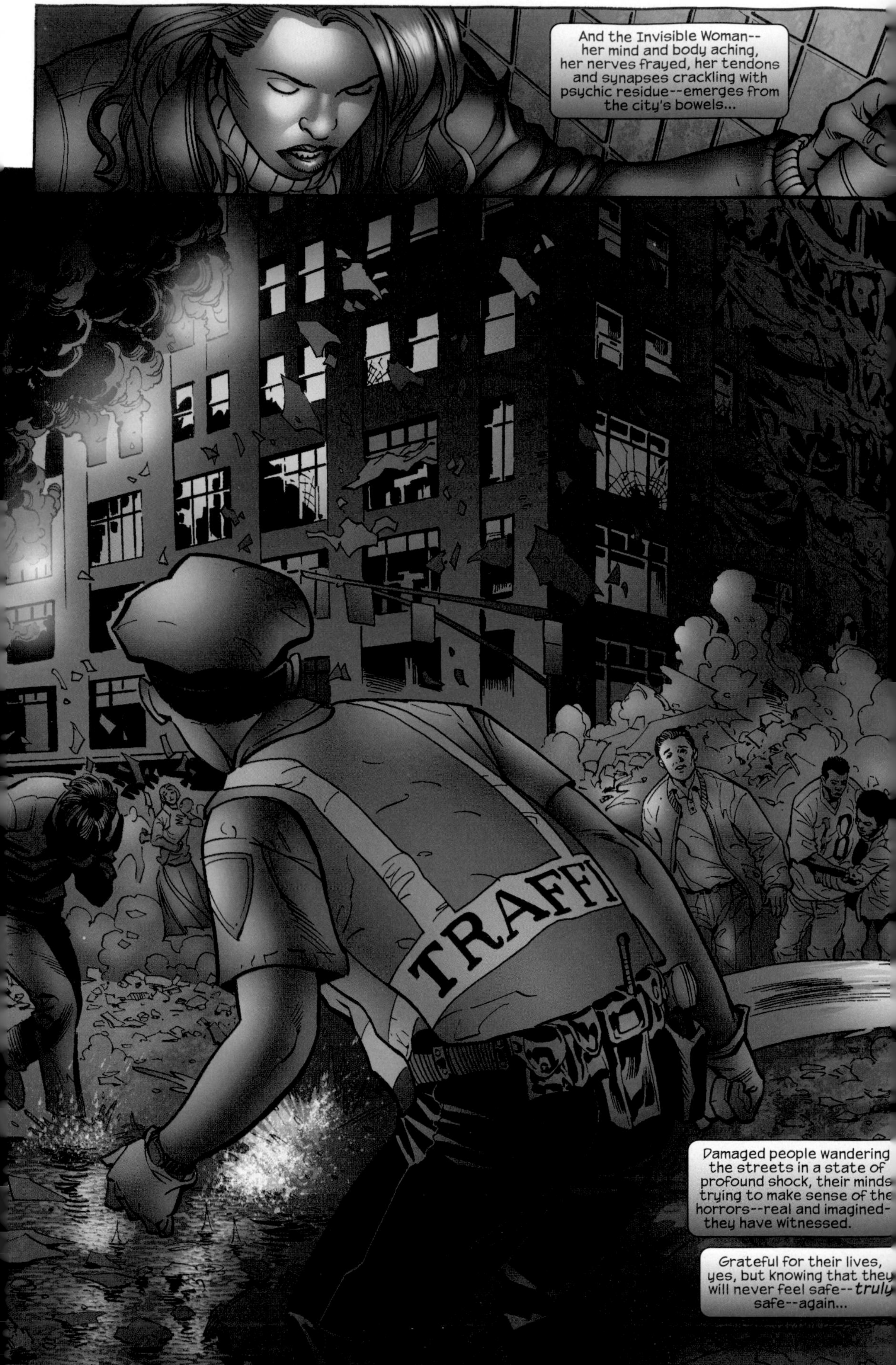
And the Invisible Woman--her mind and body aching, her nerves frayed, her tendons and synapses crackling with psychic residue--emerges from the city's bowels...
TRAFFI
Damaged people wandering the streets in a state of profound shock, their minds trying to make sense of the horrors--real and imagined--they have witnessed.
Grateful for their lives, yes, but knowing that they will never feel safe--*truly* safe--again...

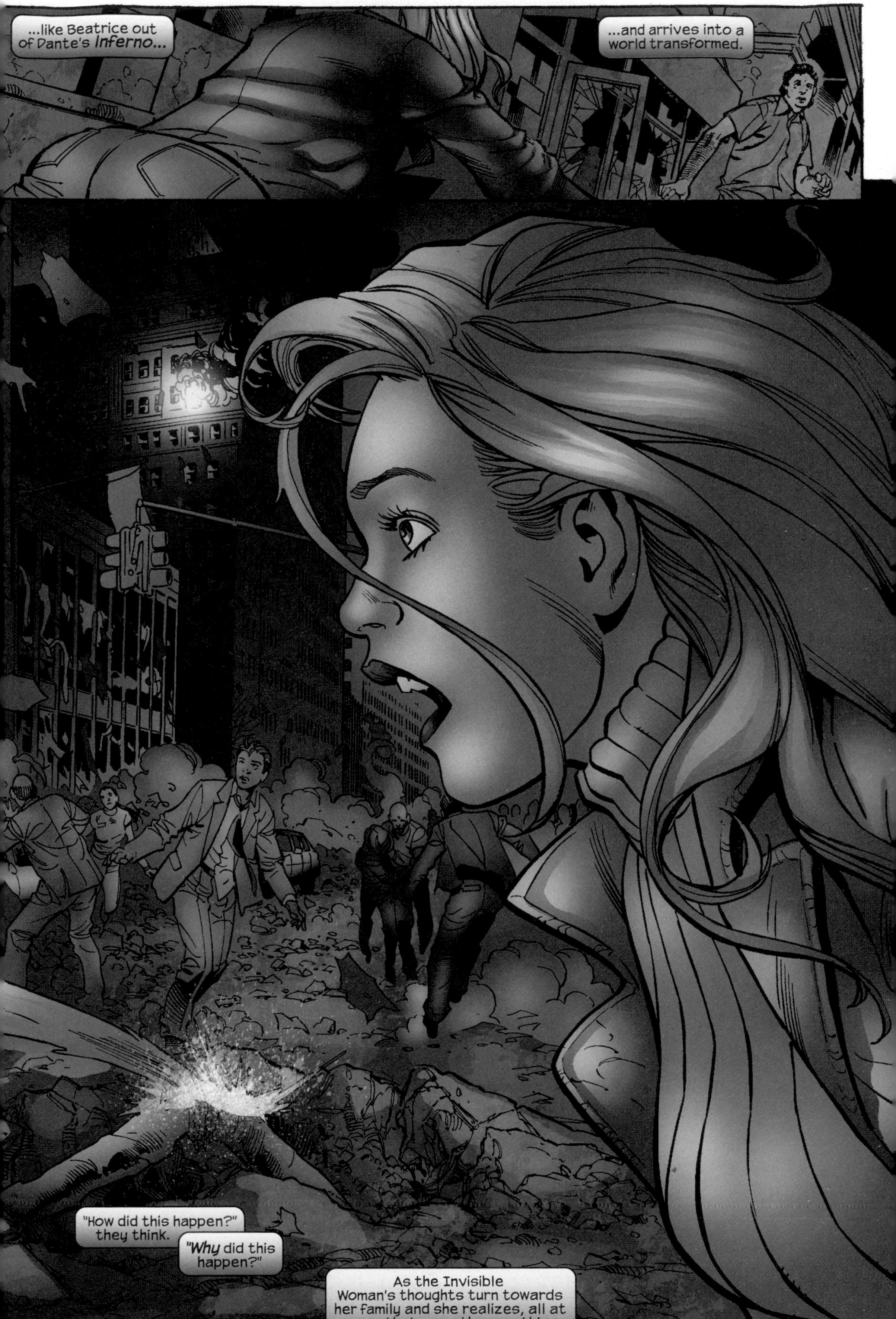

...like Beatrice out of Dante's *Inferno*...
...and arrives into a world transformed.
"How did this happen?" they think.
"*Why* did this happen?"
As the Invisible Woman's thoughts turn towards her family and she realizes, all at once, that more than anything else, she wants to be with them...

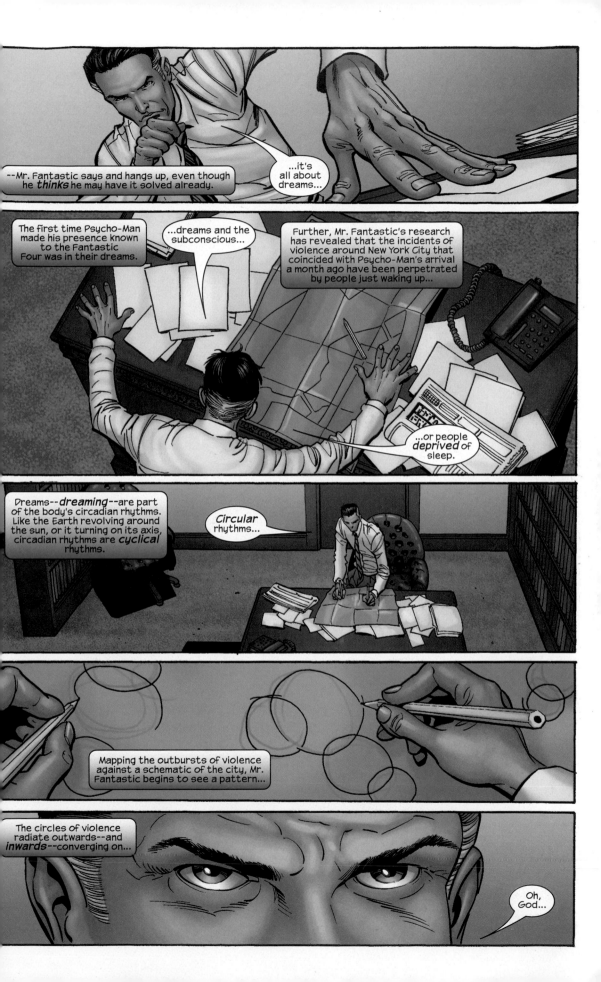

--Mr. Fantastic says and hangs up, even though he *thinks* he may have it solved already.

...it's all about dreams...

The first time Psycho-Man made his presence known to the Fantastic Four was in their dreams.

...dreams and the subconscious...

Further, Mr. Fantastic's research has revealed that the incidents of violence around New York City that coincided with Psycho-Man's arrival a month ago have been perpetrated by people just waking up...

...or people *deprived* of sleep.

Dreams--*dreaming*--are part of the body's circadian rhythms. Like the Earth revolving around the sun, or it turning on its axis, circadian rhythms are *cyclical* rhythms.

Circular rhythms...

Mapping the outbursts of violence against a schematic of the city, Mr. Fantastic begins to see a pattern...

The circles of violence radiate outwards--and *inwards*--converging on...

Oh, God...

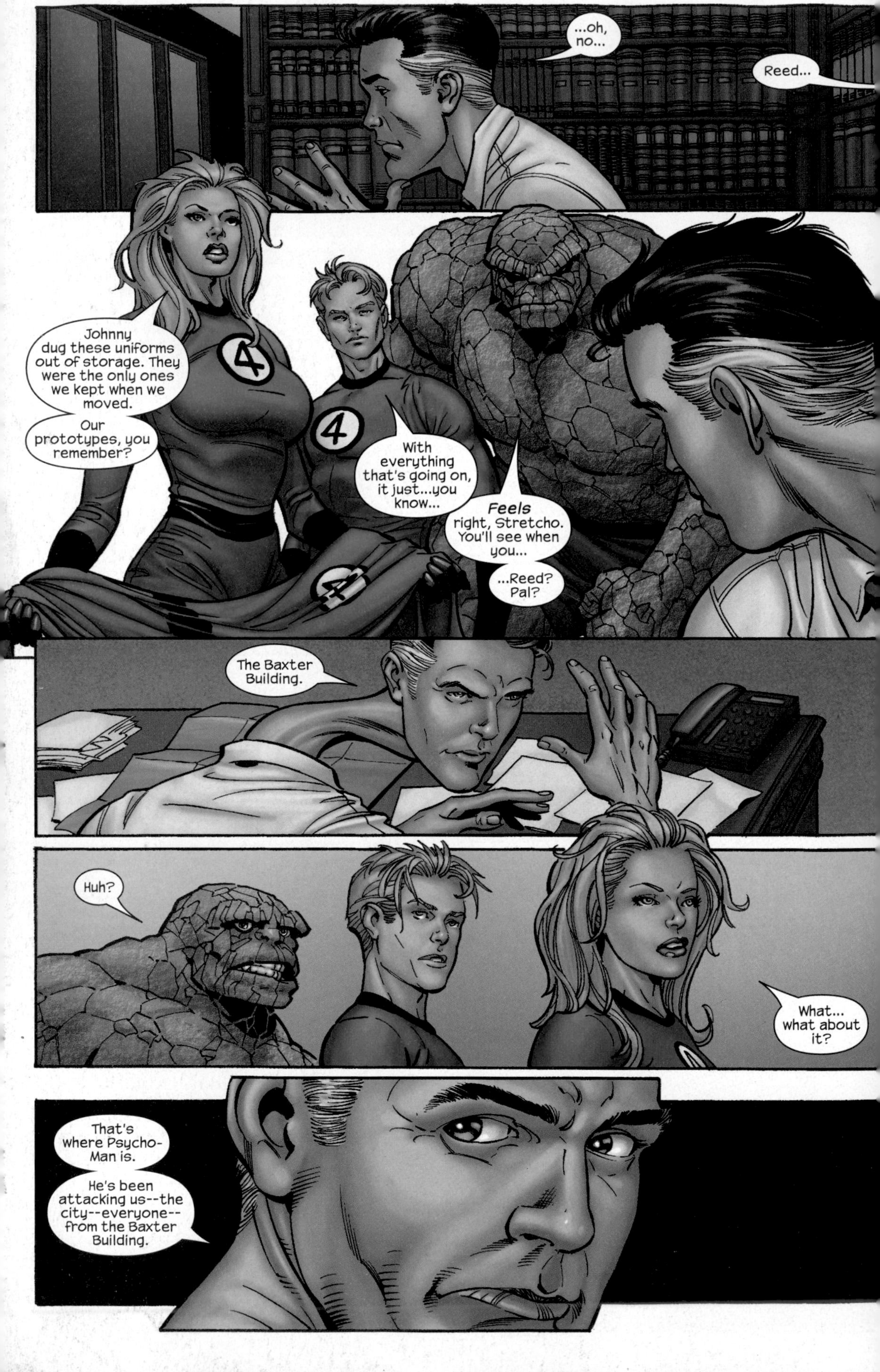
...oh, no...
Reed...
Johnny dug these uniforms out of storage. They were the only ones we kept when we moved.
Our prototypes, you remember?
With everything that's going on, it just...you know...
Feels right, Stretcho. You'll see when you...
...Reed? Pal?
The Baxter Building.
Huh?
What... what about it?
That's where Psycho-Man is.
He's been attacking us--the city--everyone--from the Baxter Building.

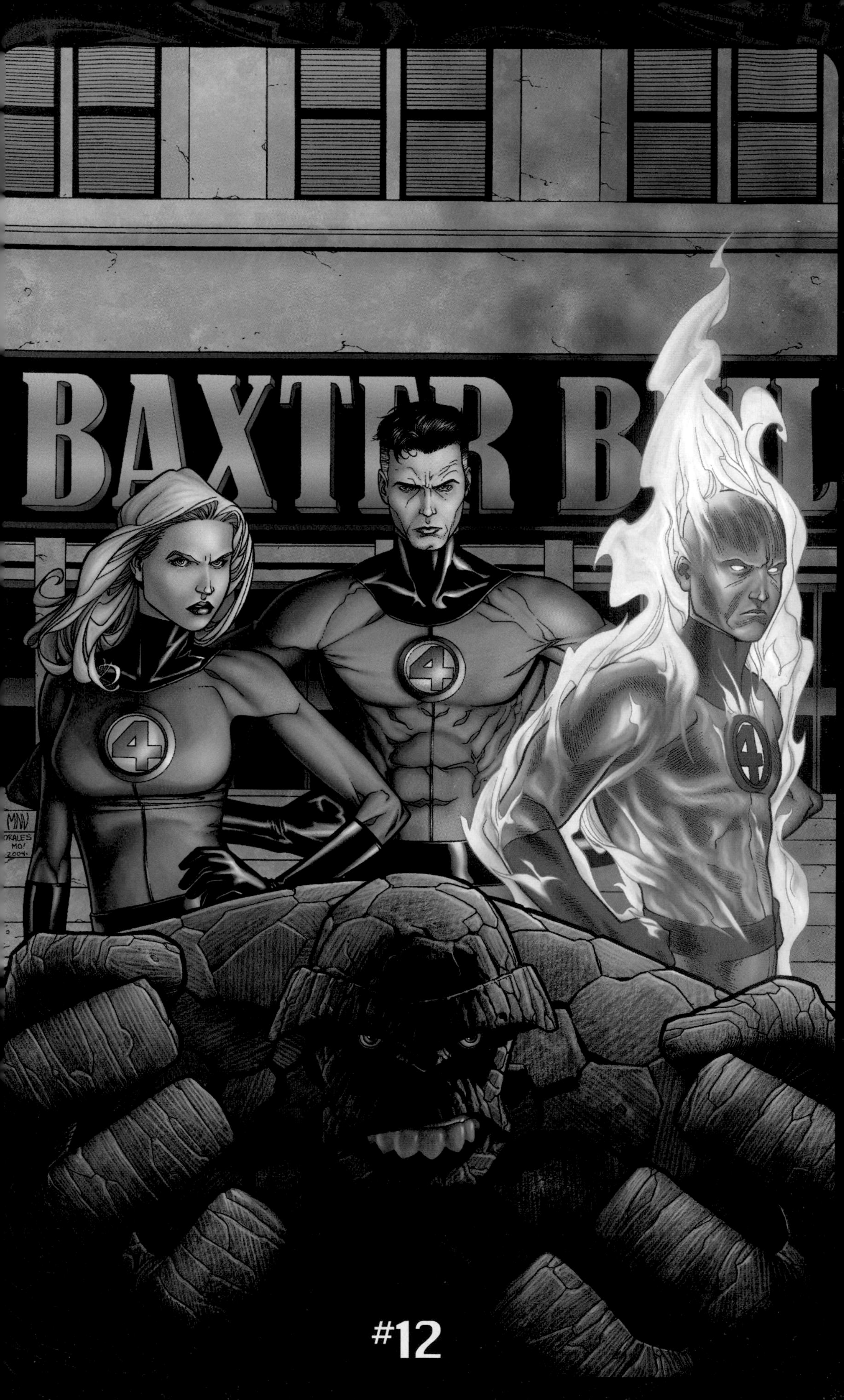
BAXTER
#12

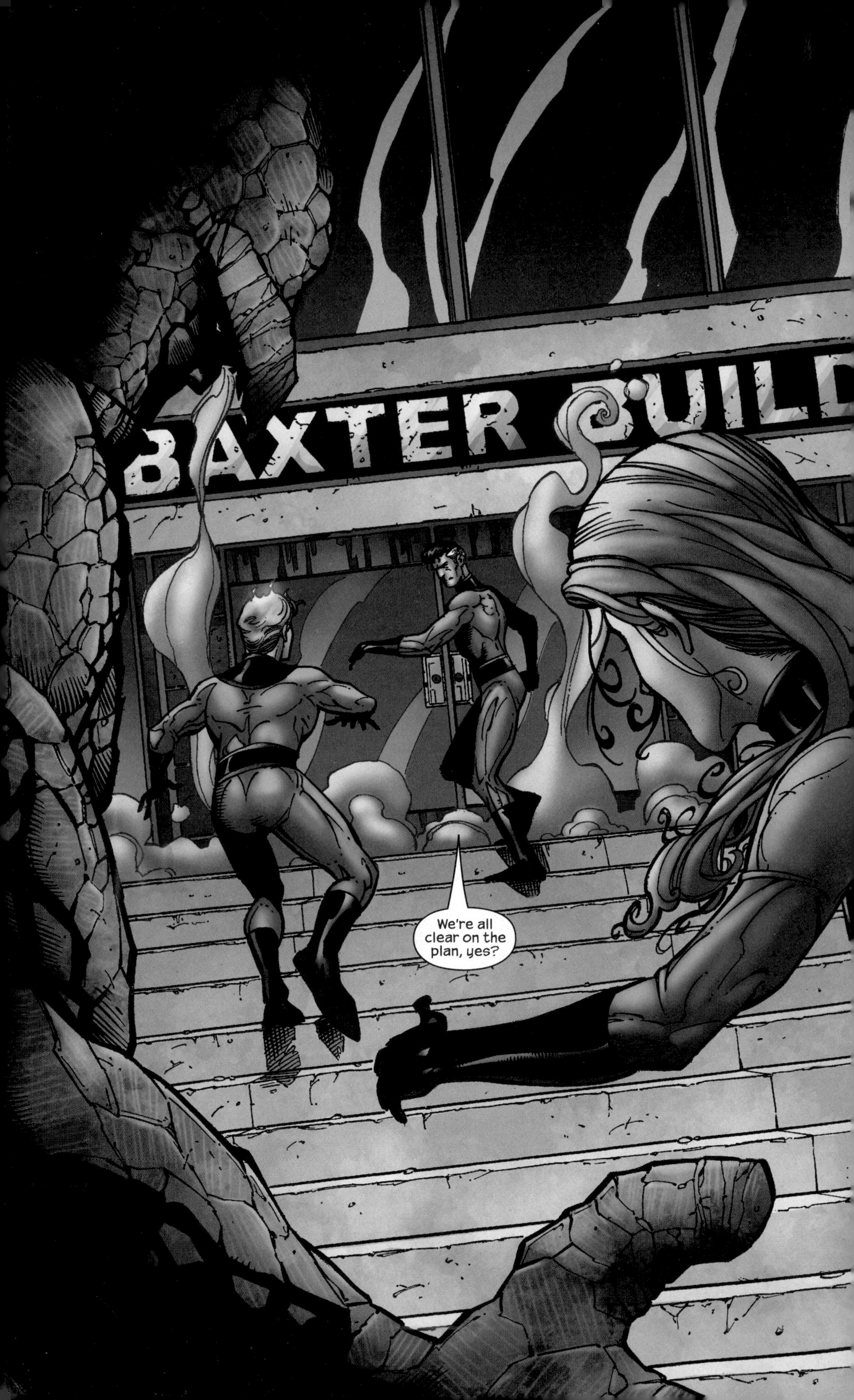
BAXTER BUILD
We're all clear on the plan, yes?

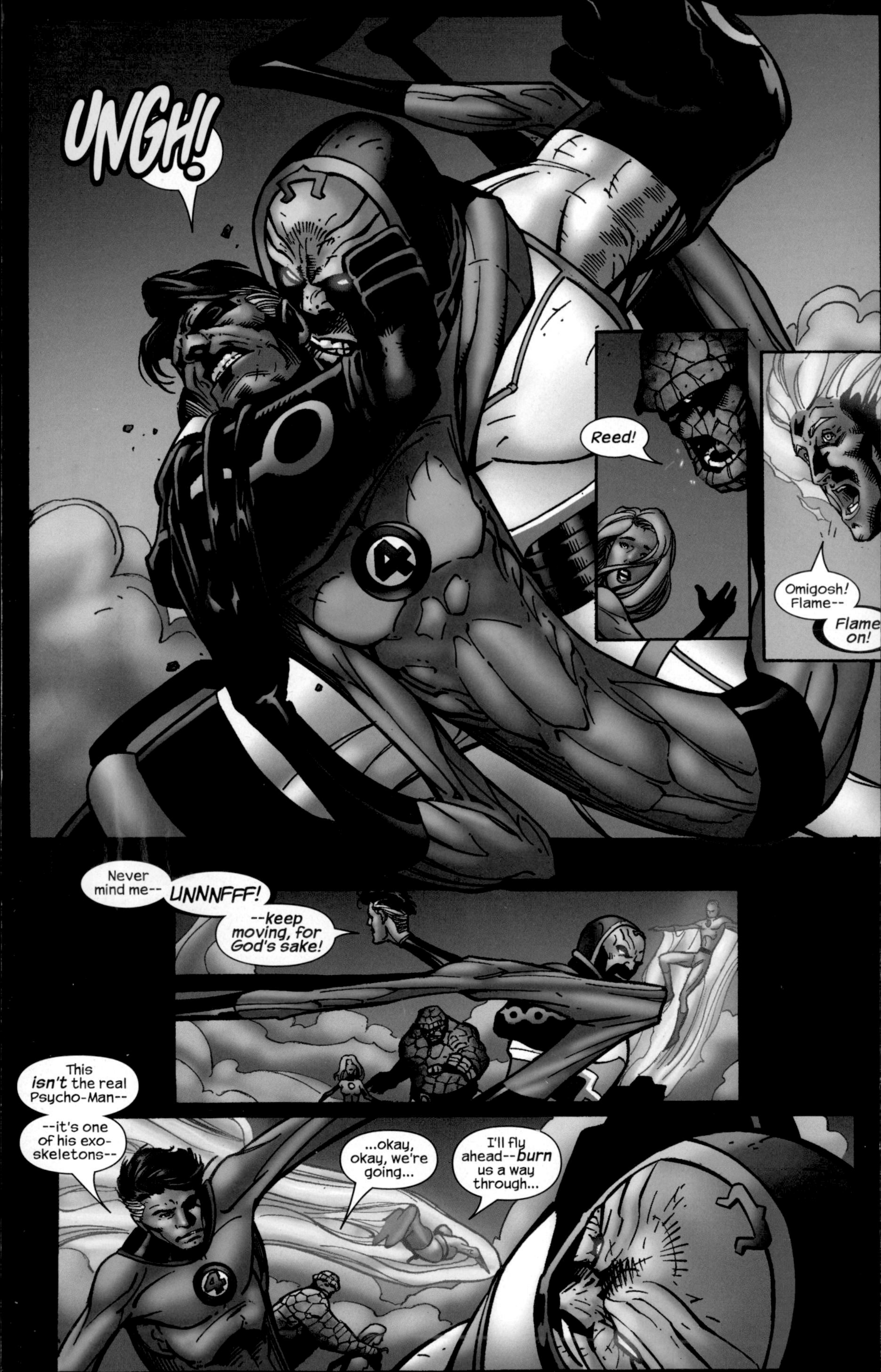
UNGH!
Reed!
Omigosh! Flame--
Flame on!
Never mind me--
UNNNFFF!
--keep moving, for God's sake!
This isn't the real Psycho-Man--
--it's one of his exo-skeletons--
...okay, okay, we're going...
I'll fly ahead--burn us a way through...

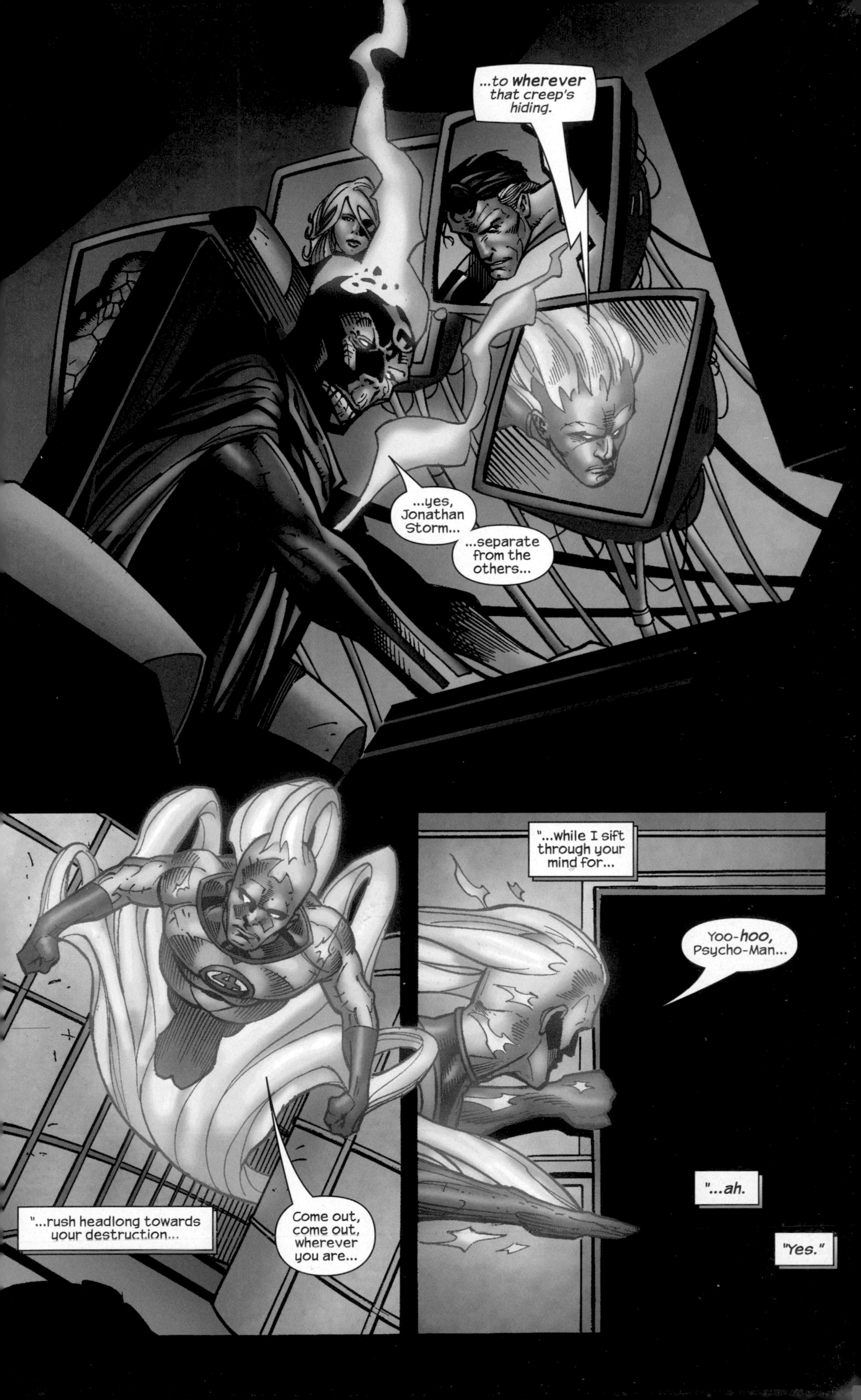
...to wherever that creep's hiding.
...yes, Jonathan Storm...
...separate from the others...
"...rush headlong towards your destruction...
Come out, come out, wherever you are...
"...while I sift through your mind for...
Yoo-hoo, Psycho-Man...
"...ah.
"Yes."

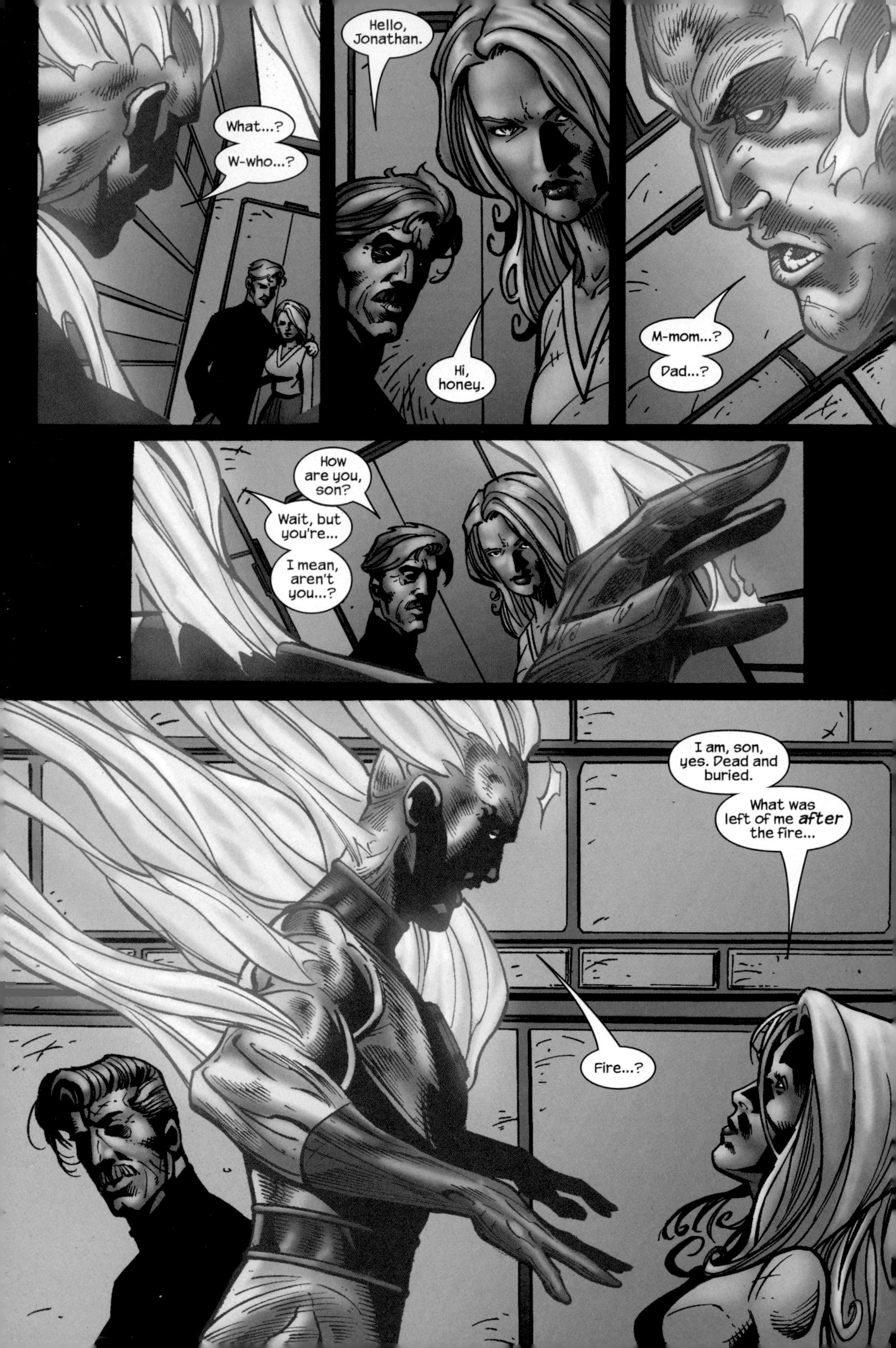
What...?
W-who...?
Hello, Jonathan.
Hi, honey.
M-mom...?
Dad...?
How are you, son?
Wait, but you're...
I mean, aren't you...?
I am, son, yes. Dead and buried.
What was left of me *after* the fire...
Fire...?

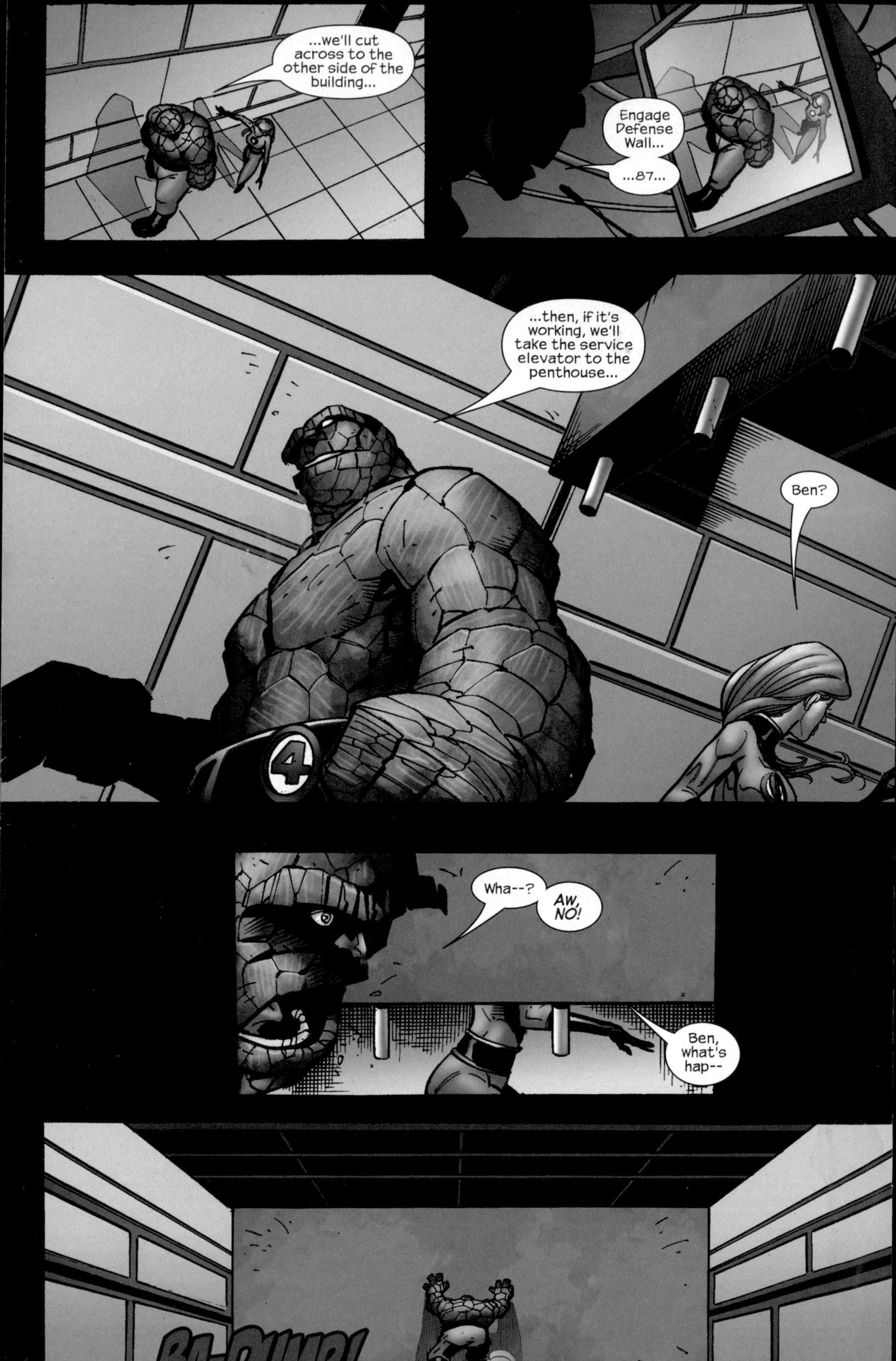
...we'll cut across to the other side of the building...
Engage Defense Wall...
...87...
...then, if it's working, we'll take the service elevator to the penthouse...
Ben?
Wha--?
AW, NO!
Ben, what's hap--
BA-DUMP!

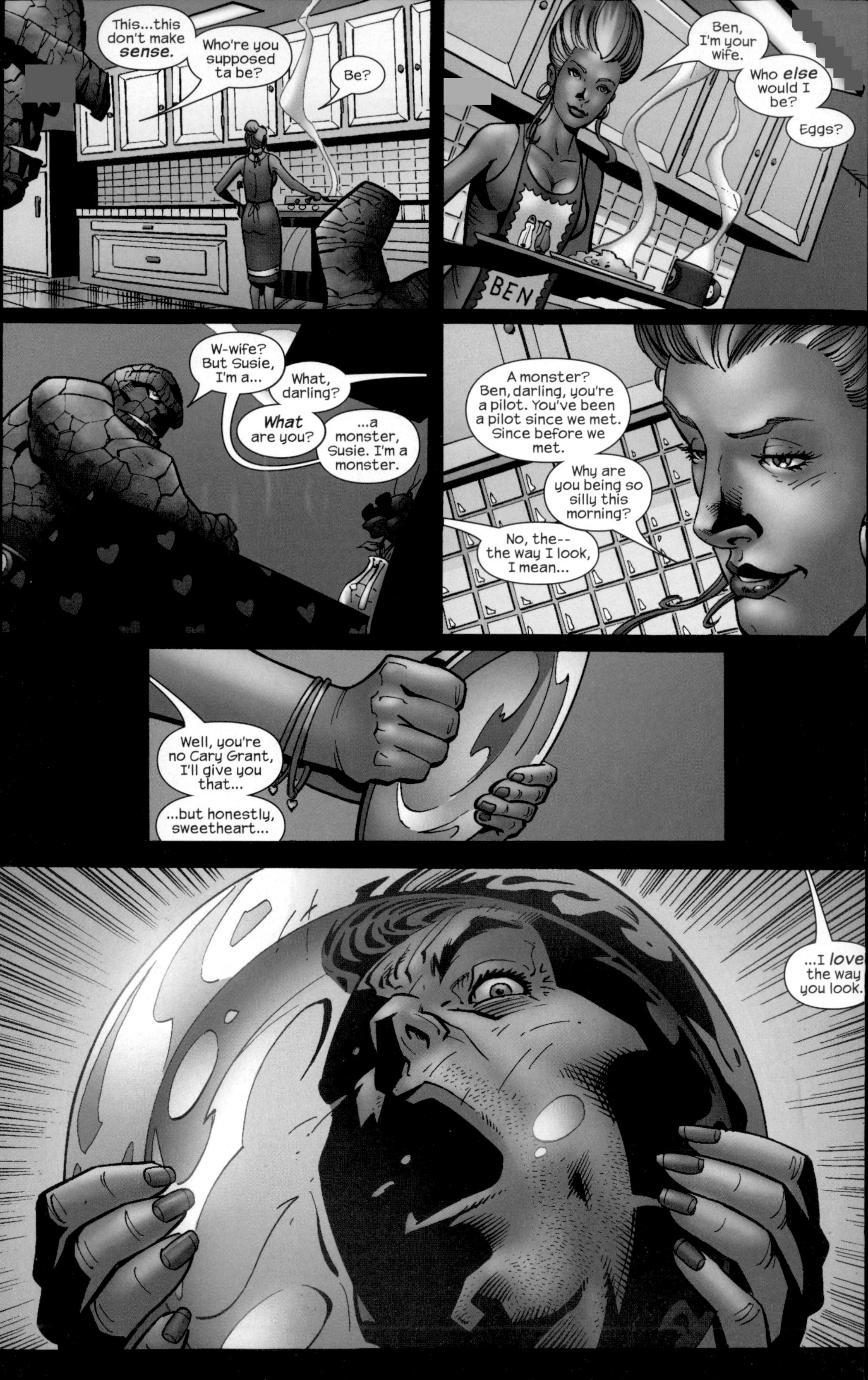
This...this don't make *sense.*
Who're you supposed ta be?
Be?
Ben, I'm your wife.
Who *else* would I be?
Eggs?
BEN
W-wife? But Susie, I'm a...
What, darling?
What are you?
...a monster, Susie. I'm a monster.
A monster? Ben, darling, you're a pilot. You've been a pilot since we met. Since before we met.
Why are you being so silly this morning?
No, the-- the way I look, I mean...
Well, you're no Cary Grant, I'll give you that...
...but honestly, sweetheart...
...I *love* the way you look.

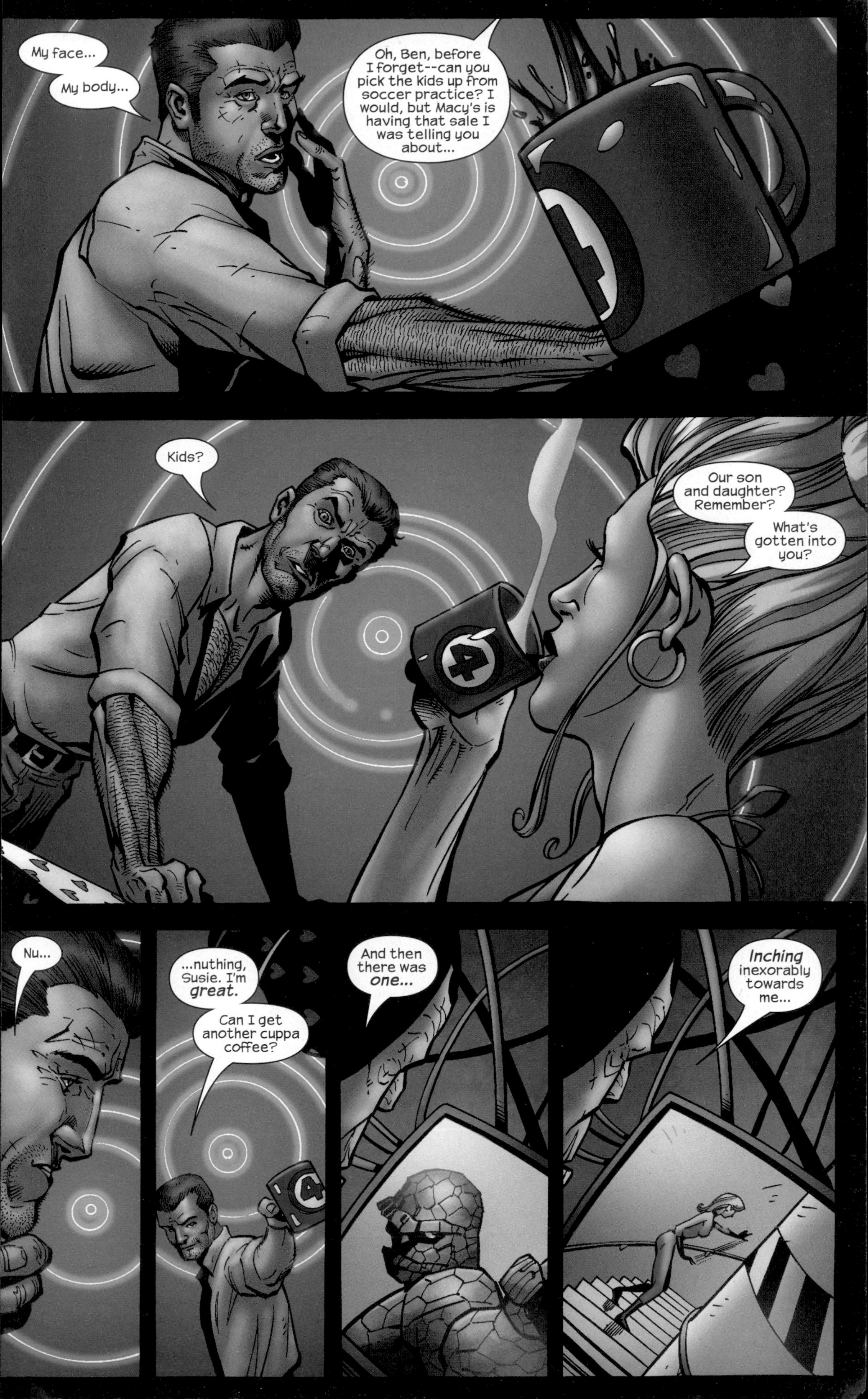
My face...
My body...
Oh, Ben, before I forget--can you pick the kids up from soccer practice? I would, but Macy's is having that sale I was telling you about...
Kids?
Our son and daughter? Remember?
What's gotten into you?
Nu...
...nuthing, Susie. I'm *great.*
Can I get another cuppa coffee?
And then there was *one...*
Inching inexorably towards me...

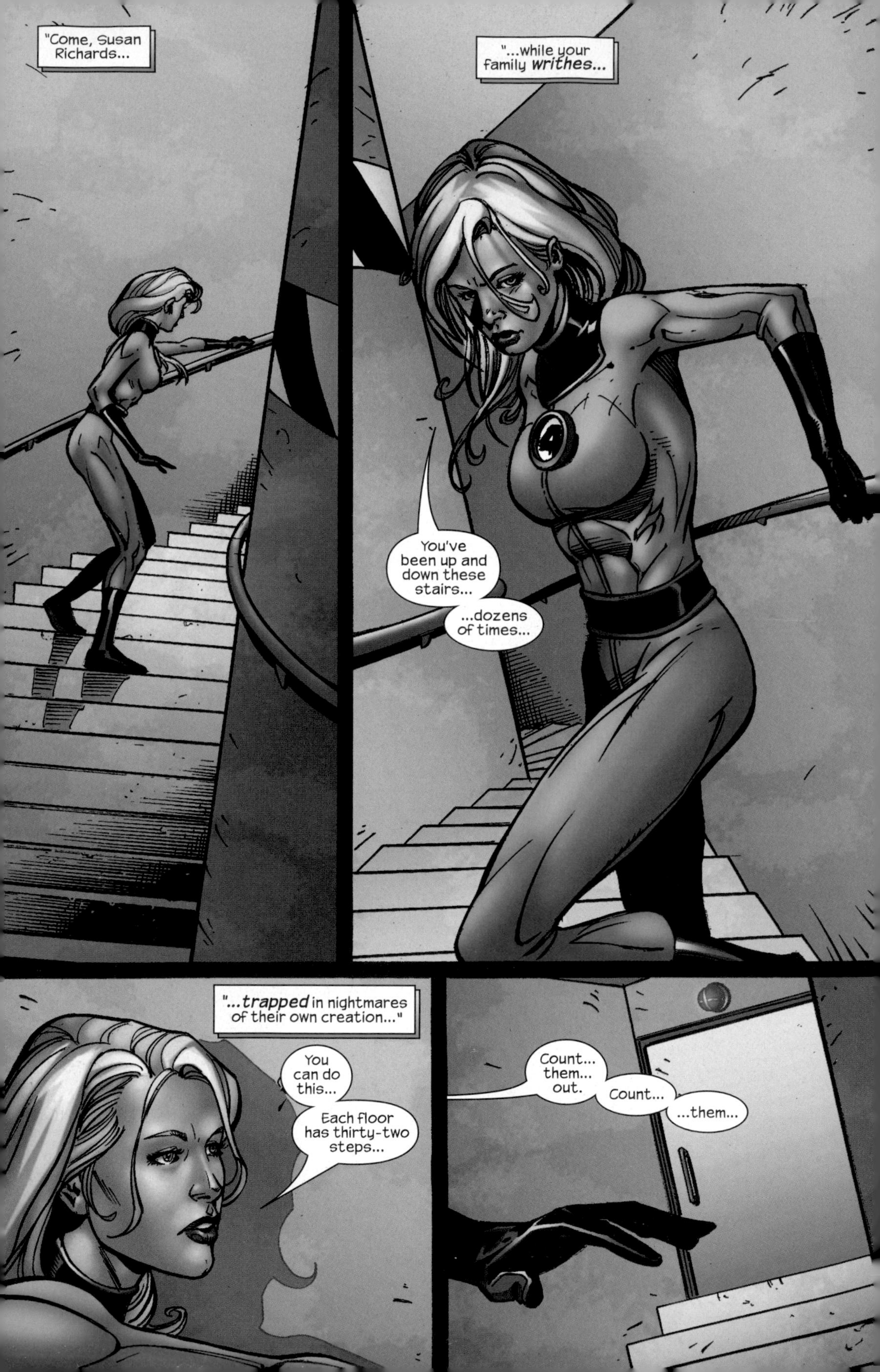
"Come, Susan Richards...
"...while your family *writhes*...
You've been up and down these stairs...
...dozens of times...
"...*trapped* in nightmares of their own creation..."
You can do this...
Each floor has thirty-two steps...
Count... them... out.
Count...
...them...

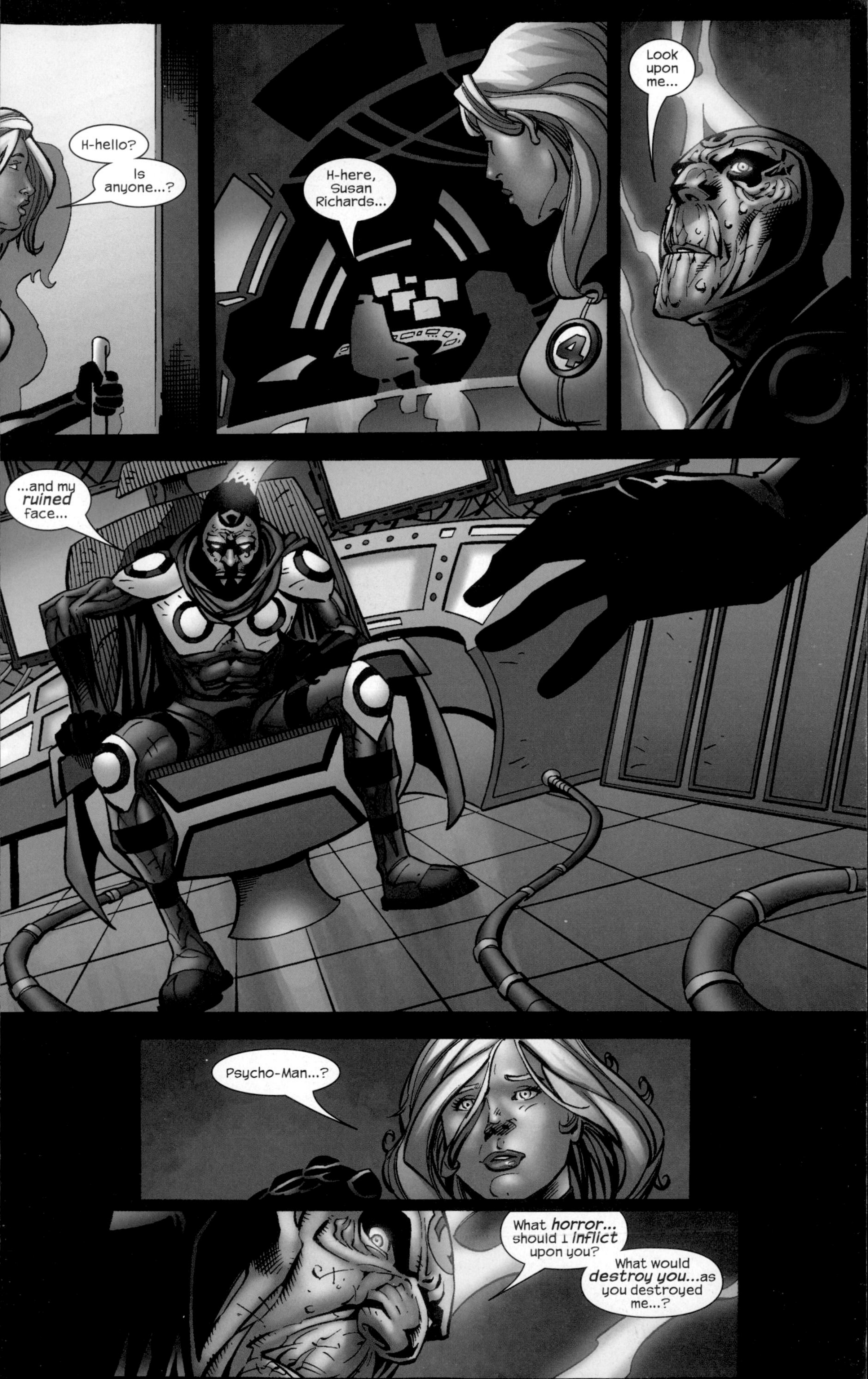
H-hello?
Is anyone...?
H-here, Susan Richards...
Look upon me...
...and my ruined face...
Psycho-Man...?
What horror... should I inflict upon you?
What would destroy you...as you destroyed me...?

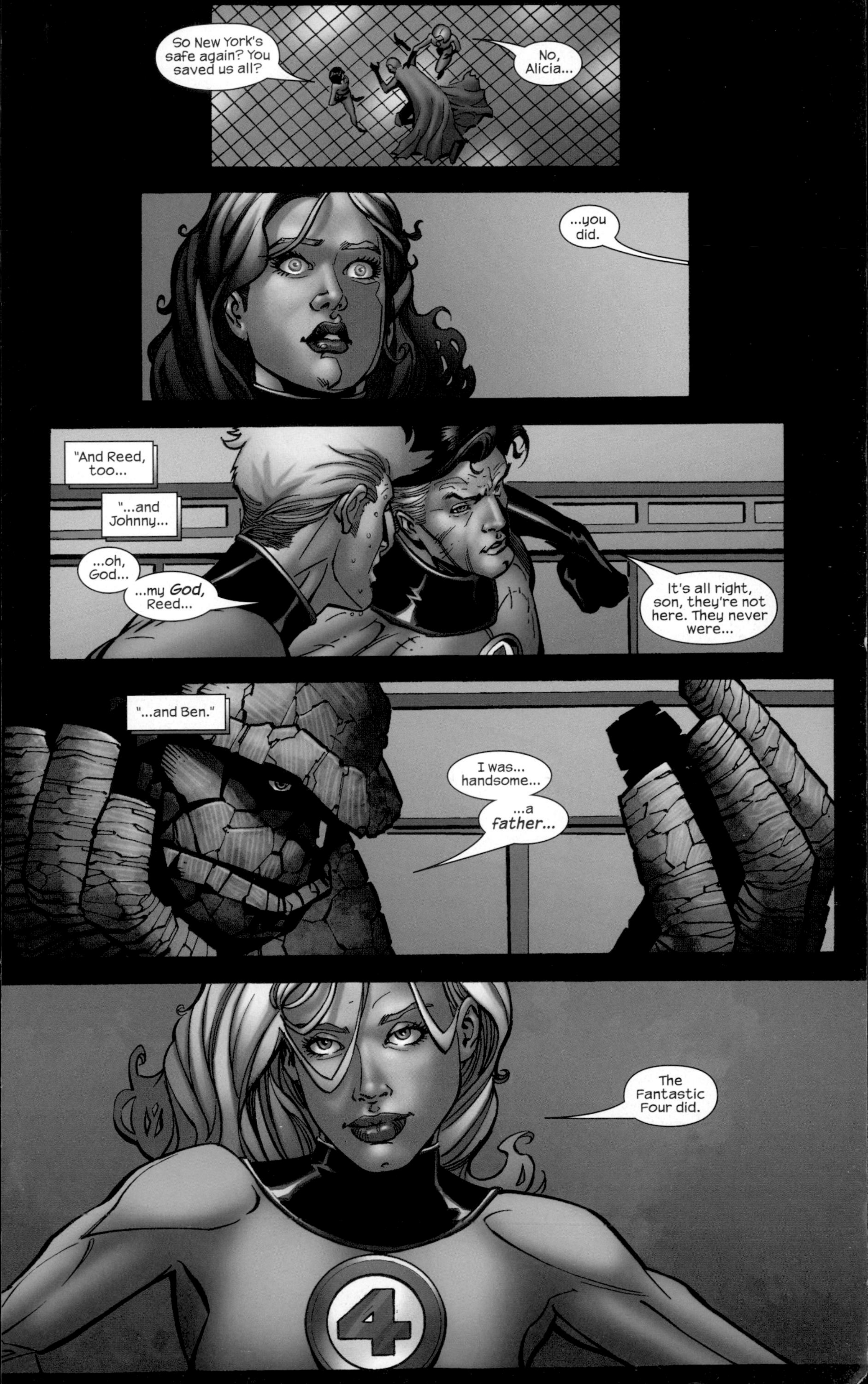
So New York's safe again? You saved us all?
No, Alicia...
...you did.
"And Reed, too...
"...and Johnny...
...oh, God...
...my *God*, Reed...
It's all right, son, they're not here. They never were...
"...and Ben."
I was... handsome...
...a *father*...
The Fantastic Four did.

Later, on the roof of the world-famous Baxter Building...

...in New York, the greatest of cities...

Reed?

Baby?

The last time we were up here was... Franklin's birthday party, wasn't it?

Not that long ago, but it feels like *ages*...

...a time of reckoning for Mr. Fantastic and the Invisible Woman...

...

What a *mess* things are, Susan...

Oh, but they're *not*, sweetie.

Psycho-Man's condition is stable and--thanks to Dr. Strange--his psychic energies have been *completely* suppressed. Tony Stark's designing him a new, *benign* exo-skeleton...

Ben and Johnny are coordinating relief efforts with the X-Men, helping to clear away wreckage...

All of the island has electricity again, more and more survivors are turning up every hour...

We're...okay, actually.

I don't mean about Psycho-Man and what he did to New York, Sue, I mean...

...

I know, sweetie.

Us, right? Our lives?

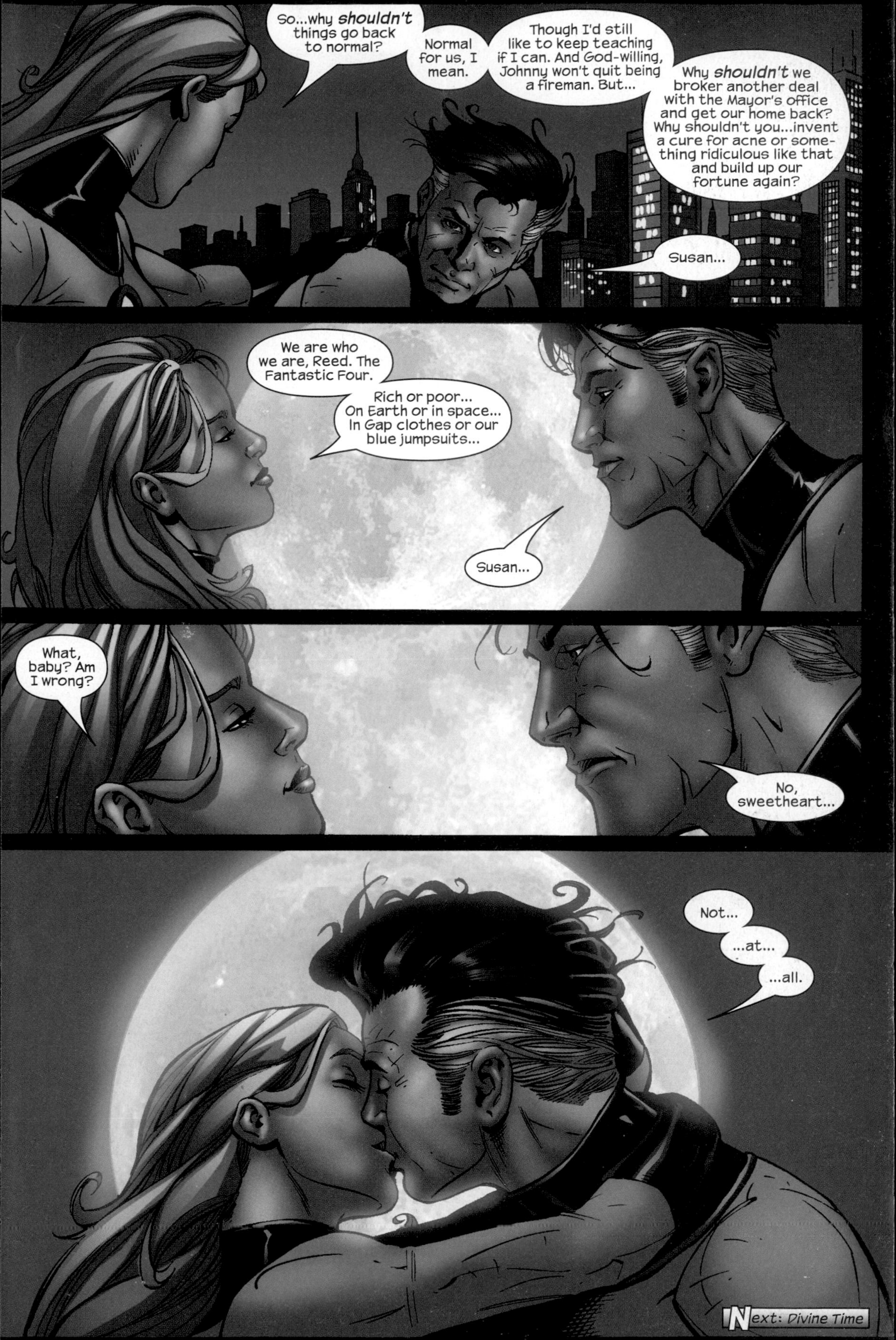

So...why *shouldn't* things go back to normal?
Normal for us, I mean.
Though I'd still like to keep teaching if I can. And God-willing, Johnny won't quit being a fireman. But...
Why *shouldn't* we broker another deal with the Mayor's office and get our home back? Why shouldn't you...invent a cure for acne or something ridiculous like that and build up our fortune again?
Susan...
We are who we are, Reed. The Fantastic Four.
Rich or poor... On Earth or in space... In Gap clothes or our blue jumpsuits...
Susan...
What, baby? Am I wrong?
No, sweetheart...
Not...
...at...
...all.
Next: Divine Time

AFTERWORD

I remember the *exact* moment I found out I was going to be working on the Fantastic Four.

It was early in May—May of 2003—and I was on my cell phone with my mom and dad, trying to convince them that they didn't need to come to my graduation later that month. "Really, it's not necessary," I was saying, when a second call started to come in.

I recognized the number immediately—a 212-576 number, burned into my brain for all eternity—since I'd been talking to Marvel, on-and-off, for a few months, pitching them on several different projects. Including one that took an offbeat, more grounded, and more human look at comicdom's First Family.

"Mom, Dad—" I said, but then just clicked over.

Marvel said some things to me, I said some stuff back, but what it boiled down to was: "We think this is great so start writing your first script, okay?"

I clicked back over. "Mom, dad—that was Marvel," I said, "Marvel Comics in New York City." (As if there were some other Marvel Comics somewhere else in the world.)

"Oh?" my mom said guardedly. (Tempering her enthusiasm the way mothers and fathers of young playwrights are conditioned to do.)

"Yeah," I said. "I'm gonna be writing the Fantastic Four for them."

Dead silence from my parents for a few seconds, then my dad said: "So I guess that means you're *not* selling those boxes of comic books in the attic?"

And then my mom said: "Sweetie, are you sure you didn't misunderstand? I remember reading 'The Fantastic Four' when I was a teenager—in Spanish. I can't imagine they'd start you out on 'The Fantastic Four.' Maybe you should call them back."

"You're right," I said, then got off the phone with them, then called Marvel again, but no...there hadn't been any mistake: My first professional comic-book-writing gig *was* going to be the Fantastic Four. (The FF's cosmic origin, remembered from a Saturday morning cartoon, started playing in my head...)

I got off the phone with Marvel and walked to my local comic book shop and told the guys there that I was going to be writing a new Fantastic Four comic book.

"*Ultimate Fantastic Four*?" they asked.

"No," I said, setting the first three *Fantastic Four Essentials* on the counter next to the cash register, "the other one." (What would eventually become *Marvel Knights 4.*)

That was almost two years ago. Now I'm writing this afterword for the second *Marvel Knights 4* collection. Truly a dream come true.

I'm as proud of the stories in this book as anything else I've written. They're dedicated to *my* Fantastic Four: my mom, my dad, my brother Raf, and my sister Georgie.

Any similarity they bear to Reed, Sue, Johnny, and/or Ben is *purely* coincidental.

Roberto Aguirre-Sacasa
December 9, 2004